3

"At one time or another every twenty-first-century Christian is likely to be confronted about his or her views on homosexuality. But how can we approach this challenging issue in a way that faithfully reflects Jesus's heart and mind? Joe Dallas answers that question in this clear and compelling guide for engaging others with both gentleness and biblical truth."

Jim Daly, president, Focus on the Family

"I've often said no one understands the subject of same-sex sexuality better than my friend Joe Dallas. This book, his best yet, only confirms my conviction. I'm not speaking merely of Joe's formidable knowledge of truth, but also the wisdom of its application through crystal-clear and concise communication. In the wake of the June 2015 US Supreme Court's redefinition of marriage, *Speaking of Homosexuality* will equip you to engage a topic that is foundational to human civilization."

Hank Hanegraaff, president, the Christian Research Institute; host of the *Bible Answer Man* broadcast

"*Speaking of Homosexuality* is one of the most clear and informative books on the subject. Dallas responds to the most common Revisionist arguments with clarity, but also genuine kindness. If you want one book to offer biblical and historical truth about homosexuality, but also how to lovingly put that truth into action, then you won't find a better book."

Sean McDowell, PhD, professor of Christian apologetics, Biola University; author, *Same-Sex Marriage* and *Apologetics for a New Generation*

"In answer to the urgency of our world's current situation, Joe Dallas has now crafted a resourceful tool filled with biblical truth and insightful strategies. *Speaking of Homosexuality* is essential for every person in need of answers for themselves, a family member, or a friend struggling with same-sex attraction."

Joni Lamb, cofounder, Daystar Television Network

D1559820

"There is no question that one of the most difficult issues facing the church today is the subject of homosexuality. But God didn't leave us in the dark on the topic of human sexuality. He gave us clear directives for this part of our lives so that we might experience the abundant life He promises. But speaking those guidelines to a confused church and a hardening culture isn't easy. No one does it better than Joe Dallas. Like no other voice I hear, Joe both lives and ministers with that continual balance of truth and love on this most contentious topic. In a day where Christians are growing more silent, we need a book like this to teach us how to winsomely engage while never retreating from God's protective Truth. This is a must-read for the church today!"

Janet Parshall, nationally syndicated talk show host

"I applaud Joe Dallas for taking on this lightning bolt of an issue in our society. He approaches the certainty of oncoming dialogue that will arise as people from all sides discuss homosexuality. I appreciate that Joe stays fixed on Scripture as his foundation for addressing this topic with love, sensitivity, and mercy."

Clay Crosse, singer-songwriter; Holy Homes Ministries

"This book is a godsend to the church. It can be a game changer. It will help our members converse intelligently about the subject with their friends, classmates, and the culture at large. We are way behind culturally and that won't change if we don't become much more intentional. Get this book!"

Bob Stith, former national strategist for gender issues, Southern Baptist Convention

"In the midst of a culture war rife with disinformation, bias, and alienation, Joe Dallas's book *Speaking of Homosexuality* disarms the hostile rhetoric and forges a bridge for genuine dialogue and understanding. The underpinning of personal experience and impeccable research qualifies *Speaking of Homosexuality* as an invaluable tool for equipping any traditional Christian to navigate the minefield of reaching out to the gay community. As a pastor of counseling, I can't think of a more powerful resource to train our counselors to become both stewards of truth and loving ambassadors who gently confront homosexuals to consider the freedom found in a relationship with Jesus Christ."

Jim McCarty, counseling pastor, Calvary Church of Santa Ana

"There is no one I trust more than Joe Dallas to address the polarizing issues of homosexuality in our culture today. Joe has a remarkable ability to integrate uncompromising biblical conviction with authentic care and compassion for people. That makes *Speaking of Homosexuality* an especially helpful resource guide—brilliantly written, comprehensive, and practical."

James Bradford, general secretary, The General Council of the Assemblies of God

"It is almost impossible in our culture today, in my thinking, to approach this topic of same-sex attraction with a successful outcome; but Joe approaches the topic in wisdom and in the loving spirit of Jesus. In my opinion, God has given in this book the right heart, correct graciousness, and the many tools to begin this much-needed journey of revealing Christ's heart to the church and the world on this most controversial issue."

Bryan Newberry, senior pastor, Calvary Chapel San Diego

"Joe Dallas brings to the reader's attention important thoughts and useful dialogue that even I—one who has worked in the field for thirty years—had not considered. In the midst of our culture's confusion, *Speaking of Homosexuality* brings clarity and truth. It provides talking points that enable us to boldly and lovingly engage in meaningful conversation, both with the gay-identified and with the gay-sympathetic. It is Must-Read-Now material for all Christians."

Jerry A. Armelli, MEd, PC, executive director, Prodigal Ministries

"Joe Dallas has a gift of bringing the truth of God's intent for people to the issue of homosexuality. His compassionate response to a most difficult subject gives caring Christians the understanding and the language to help those who might be seeking a way out of homosexuality and into new life in Jesus Christ."

Holland Davis, author; songwriter; pastor,
Calvary Chapel San Clemente

"Even though I know what I think, does the way I communicate my thoughts convey the love of Christ without compromising the truth? The wisdom found within these pages will go far in conveying the truth in love to a generation in dire need of answers. My personal hope is that every believer in America would get a hold of the concepts Joe Dallas shares in this book. I highly recommend this book as a guide for navigating the rough and tricky waters of relationship with gay/lesbian loved ones."

Dennis Jernigan, contemporary Christian
singer-songwriter; author

"Thank you, Joe Dallas, for so wonderfully addressing many of the blind spots Traditionalists such as myself face. Thank you for being so balanced, yet uncompromised biblically. Thank you for being a gift to this age and church with your insight and wisdom!"

Steve L. Powell, district secretary, Pen Florida
District Council of the Assemblies of God

"With up-to-date research and way-beyond-cliché argument, Joe offers another option—expressing Christ's compassion without sacrificing the hope only the Good News holds for transforming our inner brokenness in our dialogues with others about this 'front page' social issue. Several of the chapters would be easily worth the price of the book just for their stand-alone content. Every Christian, particularly those in kingdom leadership roles, who desires to say the right words in the right way ought to read it!"

Rev. Steve Williams, senior pastor, NorthPointe
Community Church, Fresno, California

"Joe Dallas has been one of our go-to experts for years on the topic of homosexuality. In his latest book, *Speaking of Homosexuality*, Joe addresses the most important issues in his grace-filled, winsome manner, while providing cogent and theologically sound answers for each situation. This must-have handbook will help direct your conversations, allowing truth to be revealed while keeping important relationships intact. Well done and so needed!"

Carrie Abbott, president, The Legacy
Institute; radio host; speaker; author

"How do I speak with compassion and clarity about homosexuality? In this book you will find the answer from a true Christian apologist speaking in twenty-first-century English. Joe Dallas's love for all people is at the root of each response he provides to each argument. With the wisdom of a man who has 'been there and done that' for three-plus decades, Joe Dallas presents a rational response to the difficult arguments presented by a pro-gay world."

Rick Kardos, founder and executive
director, the Nathan Project

"Christians often lack the understanding for replying to inquiries regarding homosexuality. This book provides valuable insight on how to respond when asked difficult questions. Joe Dallas offers a balanced and compassionate way to tackle these difficult situations. I highly recommend this book as a valuable resource for the wisdom necessary in discussing the topic of homosexuality in our current culture."

Rev. Bob Ragan, director, Regeneration Ministries

"In a world where cultural contexts are changing and heated conversations are shifting regarding sexuality, there needs to be a trustworthy voice that eloquently responds to the issue of homosexuality from a biblical perspective. Joe Dallas is such a voice! In *Speaking of Homosexuality* Joe equips his readers to have conversations that are accurate, caring, and faithful to the Bible. This book is a valuable tool that moves us forward in the right direction."

Bernie Cueto, PhD, associate professor of biblical and theological studies, Palm Beach Atlantic University

"Joe Dallas speaks to the core and related issues of homosexuality with accuracy, clarity, compassion and a heart to build bridges of conversation and relationship with those involved and impacted at every level. I know of no one more uniquely qualified to address this issue of massive cultural change. I have known Joe for well over forty years and believe God has raised him up for such a time as this."

Bill Welsh, senior pastor, Refuge Calvary Chapel Huntington Beach

SPEAKING OF HOMOSEXUALITY

Discussing the Issues with
Kindness and Clarity

JOE DALLAS

BakerBooks
a division of Baker Publishing Group
Grand Rapids, Michigan

© 2016 by Joe Dallas

Published by Baker Books
a division of Baker Publishing Group
P.O. Box 6287, Grand Rapids, MI 49516-6287
www.bakerbooks.com

Printed in the United States of America

Library of Congress Cataloging-in-Publication Data
Names: Dallas, Joe, 1954– author.
Title: Speaking of homosexuality : discussing the issues with kindness and clarity / Joe Dallas.
Description: Grand Rapids : Baker Books, 2016. | Includes bibliographical references.
Identifiers: LCCN 2016026108 | ISBN 9780801019159 (pbk.)
Subjects: LCSH: Homosexuality—Religious aspects—Christianity.
Classification: LCC BR115.H6 D358 2016 | DDC 261.8/35766—dc23
LC record available at https://lccn.loc.gov/2016026108

16 17 18 19 20 21 22   7 6 5 4 3 2 1

To every believer who knows that grace and truth
are not contradictory, and that true Christianity
will never compromise one for the sake of the other,
this book is offered with grateful respect.

CONTENTS

INTRODUCTION

To speak and to speak well are two things. A fool may talk, but a wise man speaks.

—Ben Jonson

You know what you think. But can you state what you know? Don't answer too quickly, especially when you're speaking of homosexuality. Because on this topic, perhaps more than any other, we tend to be long on opinion, but short on wise response.

I should know. I've been speaking on the subject for almost thirty years, and I still don't have it down. At times, in fact, I'm painfully aware of the gap between what I've said and what I should have said. So on some days I'd give myself a passing grade, occasionally even a high mark. But other days. . . . Well, I remember the other days all too well.

Like the time I told my close friends, in early 1984, that I no longer felt homosexuality was right in God's sight and that I was leaving the gay community. I'd been a staff member with a pro-gay church, an openly gay man, and an activist, identifying as a gay Christian, arguing for the acceptance of homosexuality. Anyone who knew me then had every right to believe I'd never change.

But my heart did change when I was turned around, pursued with gentle relentlessness by God until I took a cue from Saul of Tarsus and said, "Lord, what do You want me to do?" (Acts 9:6). I was brought to repentance and now faced the task of explaining my turnaround to my gay friends. There was no way for me to say that I now thought homosexuality was a sin without also saying, overtly or by implication, that I believed they were in sin too. It was a miserable challenge.

"I've had a, um, spiritual kind of awakening, ya know?" I stammered. "And I think I need to make changes, so I'm gonna relocate and try to start over."

"What are you saying, Joe?" they'd ask. "Are you saying the rest of us are going to hell? Are you now magically cured of your attraction to guys? Are you against us now?" And I could only respond with a deer-in-the-headlights gaze.

I knew what I believed but not how to state it.

Then there was my first hostile television interview—one of many—six years later in 1990, with a host and three other guests who held the pro-gay view and saw me as something between a Nazi and a Neanderthal. The television lights were hot but the host's tone was icy when the show began, and he frowned at me, smiled at the others, then turned back to me and asked, "So, Mr. Dallas, why are you so intolerant? Why do you shake your finger in gay people's faces and tell them they're sinners?"

By then I'd been ministering for a few years to people who, like me, had repented of homosexuality, and I pretty much knew, not only where I stood, but how to explain it as well. So I figured I was ready. "Disagreement isn't intolerance, so your question is off base. I hold the view that God made us male and female, and that our anatomy testifies to a certain plan when it comes to sex. And that's a plan homosexuality, by its nature, can't fulfill. Believing in that hardly makes me intolerant."

So far, so good. Then came the hurricane, blown at me from all four of them: "So who appointed you God's spokesman?" "What about hermaphrodites who are born with male and female genitals?" "What about the studies showing homosexuals might be born that way?" "Don't you know that forty years ago people like you were talking about 'God's plan' for racial segregation, and that they quoted the Bible to support their view, just like you're quoting it today?"

Sputter, stutter, gulp—another deer, different spotlight. This time I knew how to *articulate* my beliefs but not how to *defend* them.

It wasn't long before I also faced the crucible of addressing a university auditorium full of gay activists. The event was promoted by fliers around campus that announced "Joe Dallas Will Explain to You Why You Don't Have to Be Gay."

With publicity like that the outcome was predictable. Activists in black T-shirts packed the hall, and every time I opened my mouth I was interrupted with jeers, whistles, and irrelevant questions. I tossed back answers and quips for every off-the-wall interruption, and if I say so myself, my answers were pretty darned good. But within ten minutes I'd had it. I was being bullied. And having zero respect for bullies, I lost it and roared, "If you people can't act like adults, then to hell with it. I'm leaving!"

I stomped off the stage. They (amazingly) yelled for me to come back, then withheld their interruptions while I finished speaking through gritted teeth. By evening's end we'd all acted like noisy children, I being the noisiest, and to the best of my knowledge absolutely nothing of value was accomplished.

I knew how to defend my beliefs, but not with the right attitude.

Today believers holding the traditional view of marriage and sexuality often find themselves in similar situations. We may know what we believe without knowing how to articulate it. Or we may be able to articulate our beliefs without having a clue how to defend them. Or our attitude, whether fearful or antagonistic, may need some adjustment.

That's why I've written *Speaking of Homosexuality*. It's based on a Traditional perspective, so this is by no means an unbiased look at the pros and cons in the gay debate. I believe homosexual acts, like numerous other sexual behaviors, fall short of God's intention and are therefore sins. I further believe the homosexual orientation—the deeply ingrained erotic or romantic response to the same sex—is an unnatural condition God never intended, but which exists as one of many manifestations of fallen human nature, or "the flesh," as the apostle Paul often termed it. All of which makes me a Traditionalist, who has written a book specifically for other Traditionalists (as opposed to a Revisionist, who advocates revising our view of Scripture or of morality in general to condone homosexuality).

I've written this book with a twofold goal: to help the reader better understand arguments in favor of homosexuality, and to equip him or her to meet those arguments with responses that are accurate, biblical, and compassionate. That's what effective dialogue is made of, and at the risk of sounding self-serving, I believe the need for a book enhancing this dialogue is huge. Because, of all the controversies facing the modern Christian, this one seems the toughest to discuss rationally.

We may know what we believe, based on our view of the Bible as inspired by God and authoritative in all areas of life, and on our understanding that it condemns all sexual coupling apart from a male-female marriage covenant. That much may be clear. What can be unclear is how best to say what we believe when entering the national conversation about homosexuality.

Many of us have gay loved ones, and we yearn to talk about this without alienating them. Plenty of us have lesbian friends whom we respect and value, with whom we'd love to have a constructive discussion, but we wonder where to begin. Some of us are pastors who want to preach the full counsel of God without needlessly hurting parishioners who struggle in this area. And any number of us work with gays and lesbians, so when the subject of religion and sexuality comes up, we'd love to jump in. But how?

The subject is on our minds; getting it out of our mouths is another matter. *Speaking of Homosexuality* is designed to help the process along.

The Frightened

> O calm, vile, dishonorable submission!
> —Shakespeare, *Romeo and Juliet*

Many of us cave because we're scared. (I'm tempted to add the old joke, "You're not paranoid. Everyone really *is* out to get you!" because it applies.)

There's a price to pay for holding the Traditional view, and like most prices, this one's going up. Just consider three recent examples of public figures and private citizens who've expressed a conservative position on homosexuality:

- In 2013 reality TV star Phil Robertson, patriarch of the *Duck Dynasty* clan, stated his Traditional beliefs about homosexuality in an interview with *GQ*. Reaction from the cultural elite was swift and furious. Bill O'Reilly, normally considered a friend to conservatives, accused Robertson of judging.[1] A&E Network promptly suspended Robertson from the show (then quickly reinstated him in light of enormous public protest),[2] and actor Charlie Sheen publicly called him out as a "Mallard brained . . . shower-dodger" who was "sub evolved."[3]

- When restaurant chain Chic-fil-A's president, Dan Cathy, expressed opposition to same-sex marriage in a June 2012 interview, Boston's mayor, Thomas Menino, stated that he would not allow the company to open franchises in the city.[4] Chicago's alderman Proco "Joe" Moreno vowed to block Cathy's bid to build a store in the Windy City,[5] while Mayor Rahm Emanuel declared Chic-fil-A's values were "not Chicago values."[6] Not to be outdone, San Francisco's mayor, Edwin Lee, suggested Chic-fil-A not try to open shop in his city,[7] and a number of universities across the country proposed banning the chain from their campuses.[8]

- A Christian nurse was asked repeatedly by a lesbian co-worker what the Bible said about homosexuality. When she responded that "God does not condone the practice of homosexuality, but does love you and says you should come to Him as you are," the co-worker reported her, and she was fired.[9]

And so it goes. The list of outrages is longer than space allows, making it hard to dispute Dr. Laura Schlessinger: "If you're a liberal, anything you say is protected. If you're a conservative, anything you say is hateful."[10]

Certainly these events offend the sensibilities of fair-minded people, but the message they send does more than offend: "Be warned, because here's what happens when you dare express the wrong view of homosexuality." There's a chilling effect to all this which is, by any standard, intimidating.

There's also a more intimate, relational intimidation at play here.

Some of us seriously fear losing people over this issue, people we love and respect. We know they're gay or lesbian, and we wonder if we should say anything, or ignore the subject and simply enjoy our relationship with them. We don't want to alienate; nor do we want to ignore our responsibility as believers to speak truth. And, really, we're not sure what that responsibility requires of us. What to do?

At other times we feel backed into a corner because they, not we, keep bringing up the topic, forcing us either to state our position, to lie about it, or to cower in silence. And some of us have family members or friends who've already given us the clear ultimatum: "Change your views, or there's the door."

So this book includes suggestions for navigating those tricky relational waters and will leave the reader with guidelines for determining when and what to speak, when to refrain, and how to deal with irrational demands.

In these pages I'll argue for a reasoned boldness—reasoned, in that there's no virtue in deliberately seeking trouble, nor can we cry, "Persecution!" if we're reviled for making hostile, inaccurate, or tasteless remarks. If we can avoid trouble without sacrificing conscience, that is surely the better way.

That better way is not always available, though, and experience has shown that the most fair, gentle, balanced statement can be labeled as hate speech. That's an unavoidable reality, taking us back to Jesus's reminder that we are not above Him in the matter of unfair treatment (see Matt. 10:24–25). So my hope is that, while becoming more skilled at discussing this issue, we'll also embrace the principle of stewardship: Our reward comes, not from the response we get, but from responsibly speaking the truth in love.

The Angry

People who fly into a rage always make a bad landing.

—Will Rogers

If many of us are scared, others of us are mad. We've seen a shift in Western culture, and it's come at an astonishing pace.

Not long ago, the gay rights movement was asking that homosexual people be treated fairly and with respect. Words like *tolerance*, *pluralism*, and *diversity* peppered the slogans of that movement, and in retrospect much of what it aimed for seems only fair. Homosexuals should never have lived in fear of violence; being gay should never have made one a target of arrest or forced psychiatric treatment; most jobs have little or nothing to do with the orientation of the employee, so lesbians and gays shouldn't have had to worry about being fired solely because of their sexual preference.

The movement achieved much of what it sought. Then it morphed.

Today mere legitimization of homosexuality is hardly enough for the modern gay rights movement. It also demands, with all the subtlety of a socialist purge, the punishment of anyone objecting to that legitimization. And that demand, expressed through laws, institutional policies, and cultural icons, leaves plenty of us angry.

We're angry at the heavy-handedness of the US Supreme Court's redefinition of marriage. We're angry at the contempt spewed by celebrities toward Traditionalists, and by the way the media elite treat Traditionalists who bravely venture into interviews. We're angry at schools, supported by our tax dollars, taking it upon themselves to undermine our parenting by instructing our children on the normalcy of homosexuality, and the wrongness of those (us) who still don't consider it normal. We're angry about speech codes strangling voices of dissent on our high school and university campuses, and claiming the moral high ground as they do so.

We're angry at major cities that have hosted gay pride parades where men display their privates and women march bare-breasted, and the very police who should arrest them can be found marching a few floats behind. We're angry that Christian business owners are forced to choose between catering same-sex weddings against their consciences or facing lawsuits, fines, shutdowns, or all three.

We're angry at the party line that teaches our gay or lesbian sons and daughters that if we don't approve of their sexuality, we must hate them. We're angry over the arbitrary redefinition of the word *hate* to now apply to mere disagreement, or the word *love* to now mean "complete approval." We're angry over being compared to segregationists of the 1950s simply because we believe male-male and female-female coupling constitute something other than what our Creator intended.

We're angry, in short, at the evolution of the gay rights movement from a plea for tolerance into a demand for both approval and retribution. And since the offenses show no sign of abating, we can assume the anger will be with us awhile.

So be it, but we'd best be careful. Because our anger, no matter how justified, can induce fruitless outbursts like mine:

"If you people can't act like adults, then to hell with it. I'm leaving!" When I was a gay activist, nothing pleased my friends and me more than to hear hostile, inaccurate remarks about homosexuals by Christians. Those remarks reassured us that we were right, the church was wrong, and conservatives did, indeed, hate us.

So it's never enough just to hold the right position. We also have to hold the position rightly, and this book will have plenty to say about that too.

And the Rest of Us

> I'm learning how to pick my battles, and fighting with you isn't one of them.
>
> —Author unknown

Then there are the rest of us, who are neither scared nor angry, just a little bewildered. Homosexuality isn't a big deal to us; in fact, we could name plenty of social and theological issues of far greater importance. We know where we stand but have no interest in pressuring others to share our views. We get along well with homosexuals and heterosexuals alike and see no reason to create needless tension in our relationships.

But we likewise don't want to be pushed or coerced, and when the subject comes up, we want to be prepared to discuss it.

We treat our position on homosexuality like the biblical concept of hell. We believe in it, and we take Jesus quite seriously in His descriptions of a literal place of torment. We take seriously John's declaration in Revelation that those whose names aren't found in the Book of Life will be cast into the lake of fire, so that those who've not been born again will be eternally and horribly separated from God. We feel no compulsion to bring up the topic without good reason, but we'll discuss it as circumstance and discretion dictate. If pressed to state our position, we will.

So with homosexuality. We prefer neither to impose biblical doctrine needlessly, nor to apologize for it. But realistically, it will come up at times, especially when people realize we're Christians. As with the subject of hell, we feel no compulsion to bring up this topic without good reason, but we'll discuss it as circumstance and discretion dictate.

That, too, is why I wrote *Speaking of Homosexuality*.

Since truth matters, we want to be good stewards of it, part of which means preparation. Being "always . . . ready to give a defense" (1 Pet. 3:15), "ready in season and out of season" (2 Tim. 4:2), and "able to teach, patient, in humility correcting those who are in opposition" (2:24–25) means knowing in advance what to say and how to say it. Not as a memorized speech, of course, and always allowing for flexibility and inspiration. But being prepared through study and reflection is surely also part of what Paul implied when he exhorted, "Be diligent to present yourself approved to God, a worker who does not need to be ashamed, rightly dividing the word of truth" (2:15).

George Orwell said, "In a time of universal deceit, telling the truth is a revolutionary act."[11] It's self-evident that you live in a world in which homosexuality is widely practiced, growing in acceptance, and constantly discussed. You'll be called to give an answer for where you stand on it, and why you do or don't approve of it. Speaking the truth on this subject will make you, as Orwell predicted, guilty of a revolutionary act. But such a revolt is in the best tradition of the faith.

So these chapters will hopefully provide a worker's preparation to speak effectively.

The opening chapters provide a contextual overview of our conversations about homosexuality (chap. 1), a look at the kinds of people we're likely to engage (chap. 2), and guidelines for a constructive conversation (chap. 3).

I'll then walk you through ten topics that people are likely to raise in connection with homosexuality (chaps. 4–13). Each chapter consists of four components:

- The Traditional position
- Revisionist, prohomosexual arguments
- Traditionalist responses
- Summary talking points

Then our last chapter will review what Scripture has to say about stewarding truth.

Why Bother?

There are good reasons for becoming an Orwellian revolutionary, or a Pauline worker, whichever you prefer.

First, let's remember that God has already prepared the work He intends us to complete here on earth (see Eph. 2:10), including the extraordinary task and privilege of representing His heart and mind on any given topic. Ideally, then, if a nonbeliever wants to know what God thinks about a certain behavior or group, he should receive an accurate reading— from our words and by observing our behavior—of God's opinion. Which places tremendous responsibility on us. Ambassadors represent their sender, not themselves, so they'd best be thoroughly briefed, displaying nothing short of the proper attitude.

Second, we hope not only to present our case but to present it persuasively. We can take comfort knowing we've spoken truth responsibly no matter the outcome, but the outcome does matter. We want to see hearts softened, actions changed, lives transformed. And I can testify firsthand that all of these hopes can find fulfillment, and that sowing the Word responsibly is never in vain. There are always people whom God has prepared, ready to receive His purpose for their existence. Someone is waiting for you to lead them, gently, to the very outcome you crave for them.

Finally, we hope, "if it is possible, as much as depends on you, [to] live peaceably with all men" (Rom. 12:18). Our gay and lesbian friends, loved ones, co-workers, and fellow citizens may not respond to truth as we'd want, but they can at least come to better understand us and our position, especially as we in turn come to better understand them. That alone, and the goodwill it generates, can make this dialogue well worth the effort.

What an honor to seek and discover God's heart and mind, as revealed in His Word. Since Scripture is so key to this discussion, let's begin by remembering we're commissioned to learn the truth, live that truth, and express that truth, and the Heart it reflects, to whoever will hear.

By His grace, then, let's explore how we can best do all three.

1

THE CONTEXT
OF OUR CONVERSATION

Whenever you tear an idea from its context and treat it as if it were a self-sufficient, independent item, you invalidate the thought process involved.

—Leonard Peikoff, American philosopher

On June 26, 2015, the US Supreme Court struck down state laws limiting the definition of marriage to a heterosexual union. While there's no understating the significance of the decision, what followed on Pennsylvania Avenue signaled a seismic change in context as well as law.

The president, celebrating the SCOTUS decision, had the White House bathed in rainbow-colored lights, announcing that the world's most powerful leader felt the redefinition of marriage should be heralded at the highest level of government. And an unmistakable message was sent to everyone with traditional views: "We've turned a corner. Henceforward, your viewpoint will not only be considered the minority view but will require a defense as well. Change, or explain yourself."

It's in the context of this national shift that we now speak of homosexuality.

Context Changes Everything

Let's bring this down to the personal context. How would you feel if someone greeted you, "Hey, dirtbag, you're looking like a paunchy old wino. Get a facelift!"

Insulted? Outraged? Ready to fight?

Funny, I didn't feel that way at all. My buddy of more than twenty-five years greeted me with those words just a few weeks ago when I sat down to coffee with him, and far from insulted, I was delighted. His banter proved our closeness. Most men I know see teasing as playful sparring reserved for well-bonded friends. Of course, if someone I knew only casually threw a remark like that my way, I'd be furious. Words that in one context would incite hostility, when spoken within the context of long-standing friendship, spark a brotherly glow.

In conversation it's never just about content. Context—the nature of the relationship, the history the participants share, the roles they play in each other's lives, social tensions between groups to which they belong—has its effect on both dialogue and emotional responses. You can't divorce context from a conversation. It's what determines whether "Hey, dirtbag!" is an insult or a term of endearment.

It's no wonder, then, that the disciples were stunned when Jesus went out of His way to engage a Samaritan woman at a well (John 4:1–43). Asking someone for a cup of water was normal under other circumstances, but not these, considering the long-standing animosity between Hebrews and Samaritans. So while the content of His first words ("Give Me a drink," 4:7) wasn't startling in itself, in context it certainly was. So much so that, before responding to His request, she first commented on the surprising fact that they were even talking: "How is it that You, being a Jew, ask a drink from me, a Samaritan woman?" (4:9).

Knowing and remembering the context of our conversation helps us speak wisely. It reminds us of whatever preconceived ideas the other person might have about us. It keeps us sensitive to suspicions or grievances they may feel toward "people like us," and it helps us better understand the resistance (or even hostility) that can arise.

Let's not be naïve. When you, a conservative Christian, speak of homosexuality to a homosexual, you're tackling many of the same challenges Jesus faced with a Samaritan—preconceived ideas she had about Jews, bad experiences she'd had with them, things she'd been told about them (some true, some not), and an overarching awareness that her group and His group stood at odds. All of those obstacles were in place before the two of them met.

When we engage in dialogue with a gay friend or loved one, we usually have to deal with double the complications the Lord did, because, being sinless, Jesus had no prejudices or misconceptions. But we have ours, as does the other person. We can know what Scripture says about homosexuality as a behavior, but little about homosexuals as people. So they may have their preconceived ideas about us; we may have ours about them. Also part of the dialogue's backdrop is the subject's highly political nature, plus the national clashes over same-sex marriage and gay-related legislation. Additionally, most cases involve interpersonal history, whether good or bad.

Three key elements, then, shape the context of the conversation between a Traditionalist and a Revisionist (someone holding a prohomosexual viewpoint): *presumption*, *politics*, and the *personal*.

Presumptions: Ours about Them

The history of Christian writing and speaking on homosexuality is rich with presumptions, some of which, I'm sorry to say, have been mine. You'd think that I, formerly active within the gay community, would be immune to overgeneralizations. But in earlier years, I've said and written things I now see were too general, too . . . well, presumptuous.

My position on the wrongness of homosexuality hasn't budged an inch, nor will it. But now I'm more willing to answer "I don't know" to questions about its origins, allowing for the fact that no one theory of causation seems to fit every person. I'm also less adamant now about the controversial "change" issue, because history has shown that, although some people abandon homosexual behavior and find they have potential for heterosexual response, others find they remain attracted exclusively to the same sex and live celibate lives. Different people experience different outcomes, and both outcomes should be respected. (We'll tackle that in chap. 5.)

As I mentioned, I'm now disinclined to rely on any one theory about the cause of homosexuality. There are many, and I see value in many of them, but I realize that, while one theory fits one person well, it might fail to explain the experience of another. So now I'm adamant only about Scripture and willing to consider the merits of any secular theory without adopting it as universal truth.

Common Misconceptions

Many believers cannot or will not recognize that homosexual orientation (same-sex attraction) is usually involuntary. They think somehow gays and lesbians glanced over the menu—heterosexual, homosexual, bisexual—and ordered the same-sex special. Others presume all homosexuals are promiscuous, or politically liberal, or easily identified, or aggressively pushing the "gay agenda," whatever that is. They use terms like *gay lifestyle*, assuming all gays and lesbians live the same way. And they believe all gays and lesbians are activists, sharing identical social and political goals.

Other folks conclude that if the homosexual orientation is *not* a choice, then only an early molestation, trauma, or unsatisfactory father-son or mother-daughter relationship could account for same-sex desires. And perhaps most presumptive of all, they've decided that no homosexual could truly be happy. So deep inside, they tell themselves, their gay friend or loved one really wants to be straight but just isn't ready to admit it.

None of these assumptions holds true in every case, because there's as much diversity in lifestyle and experience among homosexual people as among heterosexuals. There are politically conservative and moderate gays as surely as there are liberals; some are celibate, some are in monogamous relationships, some nonmonogamous; some are occasionally active sexually, some wildly promiscuous. Some are easy to spot; others, you'd never know. Many were subjected to early traumas or faulty parenting; others sprang from healthy, loving homes. And while some are dissatisfied with their sexuality, others are content.

So to say homosexual acts are wrong in God's sight is a far cry from saying all homosexuals are cut from the same cloth. You don't have to cling to stereotypes in order to maintain the biblical view.

But that inconvenient fact won't keep misconceptions from coloring the context of conversations between gays and some obstinate

Traditionalists. Many on both sides of the debate are guilty of stereotyping. We'll address all the misconceptions cited above, but it's enough for now to recognize they exist, and they matter.

The Ick Factor

Sometimes, though, a Traditionalist's response to homosexuals is hindered less by false assumptions and more by an exaggerated emotional aversion. This is more common among men, sometimes so strong that it stunts a believer's ability to communicate with, much less relate to, a gay or lesbian. I call it the Ick Factor.

Some distaste at the image or concept of homosexual sex is to be expected and doesn't constitute homophobia but, instead, a natural aversion to unnatural behavior. But if you can't talk to a homosexual without thinking about what he does in bed, or you're morbidly focused on her sexual activities, or you classify his sexual sin apart from and above all others, that's not just a distaste for sin—that's an inflated reaction, maybe even an unhealthy fixation. If you find gay sex to be "icky," yet you keep thinking about it, like gawking at a traffic accident—repulsed and fascinated at the same time—then I'd say the Ick Factor has a hold on you.

So the problem of presumptions, stereotypes, misconceptions, and the Ick Factor all contribute (negatively) to the context of our conversation. But many homosexuals also have presumptions about conservative Christians.

Presumptions: Theirs about Us

When I was part of the gay community, my friends and I referred to the conservative church as The Enemy. We assumed most Christians harbored deep, venomous animosity toward us, evidenced in the way they spoke about us and their efforts at defeating our political goals. I suspect little has changed since then, and the few statistics available seem to confirm that.

In 2007 the Barna Group reported that 91 percent of young non-Christians believed modern Christianity was "antihomosexual" and that believers showed "excessive contempt and unloving attitudes towards gays and lesbians." As if that weren't bad enough, the same study indicated that the majority of young churchgoers felt the same way.[1] If that's the case, both nonbelievers and believers of the next generation presume Traditionalists don't love homosexuals and, in fact, hold them in contempt.

Underscoring this, the Public Religion Research Institute in 2013 determined that more than four in ten Americans gave religious organizations a D or an F in their handling of homosexuality. The same number also said they believe the messages from places of worship contribute "a lot" to negative perceptions of gay and lesbian people.[2] This led David Aikman, former *Time* correspondent and senior fellow of the Ethics and Public Policy Center in Washington, DC, to conclude, "Gays, in general, regard evangelical Christians not just as critical of them, but also as implacably hostile toward them."[3]

We can protest these characterizations, and we should. Many today interpret any objection to homosexuality, no matter how kindly voiced, as hostility, so the accusation of hatred usually misrepresents our attitude. But let's not pretend there's no reason for gays to presume we're hostile. When Christian leaders say less-than-charitable things about gays, then gays will logically assume those leaders speak for the rest of us.

When the Rev. Jerry Falwell declared AIDS was God's judgment on homosexuals,[4] considering the man's influence and huge Christian following, homosexuals had good cause to think we all agreed. When Benny Hinn, a controversial but popular faith healer, prophesied that "God would destroy the homosexual population by fire"[5] by the mid-1990s, and the entire auditorium broke into applause upon hearing that gays would die, why wouldn't gays think we were all applauding as well? When Pat Robertson accused AIDS-infected homosexual men in San Francisco of wearing rings with blades in order to cut and infect others,[6] it's inaccurate but hardly unfair for homosexuals to think plenty of us believe him. And when Donnie Swaggart, son of evangelist Jimmy Swaggart, told his television audience that gays would, if possible, employ beheading tactics to silence their enemies,[7] any gay or lesbian might well put two and two together and come up with hate.

Combine these with less-than-responsible remarks about gays by private citizens, less-than-loving comments hurled from lesser-known pulpits, and legitimate-but-misunderstood objections to homosexuality expressed by many believers, and you can see why the presumption that we're hostile is widespread. The point isn't whether those presumptions are warranted—a subject we'll discuss in chapter 7. If someone thinks we view them with disdain, fear, or outright hostility, we need to know and, when possible, counteract it.

The misunderstanding works both ways. We are at times wrong about them; they are at times wrong about us. And those wrongs can't help but cause some of them to ask, much as the Samaritan to the Hebrew, "How is it that you, a Christian, are speaking to me, a gay?"

Politics

Let's walk a mile in the shoes of the lesbian woman or homosexual man with whom we're conversing. They know we're Bible-believing Traditionalists, and they know we vote. So they don't need much imagination to guess how we vote on virtually any gay-related legislation, directly impacting their personal, economic, and professional lives.

They also logically assume we support organizations that lobby against social and political goals they hold dear (whether we support those efforts or not) and that we actively support candidates whose views are closer to ours than theirs. These are all intelligent, informed assumptions, often true, sometimes not.

In short, gay co-workers, friends, or family members can easily see us as people who directly or indirectly, through the democratic process, seek to deny them rights they feel are essential. It's understandable if they even view us with the same why-do-you-hate-me? bewilderment with which African Americans viewed white segregationists decades ago.

I'm fully aware many Christians do not, in fact, oppose all pro-gay legislation, just as I know many Traditionalists on homosexuality are not conservative Republicans and may support politically liberal candidates. But as of this writing, statistics indicate most of us who are theologically conservative are politically conservative as well, a reality all too obvious to the gay community. How then, they ask themselves, are they to trust people who would deny their rights?

For all these reasons, mistrust is a frequent companion to many a homosexual conversing with a Traditionalist.

But mistrust works both ways, because we, too, feel threatened. Some of us see the gay rights movement's political and social goals as unfair, sometimes even draconian. And whereas many lesbians and gays believe we threaten their sexual and relational freedoms, many of us believe they threaten our freedoms of speech, religion, and conscience.

As noted earlier, Christian businesses have suffered lawsuits and legal judgments for refusing to service same-sex weddings, even when other vendors providing the same services were available and willing. The academic environment on college and high school campuses is restrictive and punitive toward believers who speak their minds on the subject, no matter how respectfully. And in a number of companies or industries, Christian employees feel pressured to express open support for pro-gay causes or positions the company has adopted, of which they privately disapprove.[8] Fear of retaliation can leave them feeling paralyzed.

And that's not to mention international trends that, in some nations, show even more heavy-handedness with conservative dissidents. Many are familiar with the case over ten years ago of Swedish pastor Ake Green, who, in violation of recently enacted Swedish law, made statements from his pulpit that were deemed "damaging to people based on their sexual orientation."[9] Pastor Green served jail time, and during his trial the prosecution noted that "collecting Bible [verses] on this topic as he does makes this hate speech."[10]

Our neighbor Canada is not far behind Sweden. In 2013 the Supreme Court of Canada ruled that Bible-based expressions opposing homosexuality constituted a hate crime, upholding the conviction of activist William Whatcott for distributing flyers regarding the Bible's prohibitions against homosexuality.[11] Christian radio broadcasts, when referencing homosexuality, are often censored before being aired in Canada.[12] And I can testify firsthand to the dos and don'ts imposed on Christians when speaking over the Canadian television or radio airwaves.[13]

The list of grievances against European countries imposing limits on religious expression, especially concerning this subject, is awfully long,[14] ominously hinting at America's conceivable near future. The Traditionalist is conscious of all this when conversing with someone who's gay, lesbian, or prohomosexual, leaving both parties feeling, at times, guarded and suspicious. There's just no way for the current political landscape not to play, sometimes significantly, into the context of our conversations.

The Personal

When a young woman, intending to embrace rather than reject her homosexuality, informs her Traditionalist parents that she's lesbian, the topic is never just lesbianism. It's also individuation—the woman's need to determine her own course. Her question is not just, Will you accept me? but also, Will you allow me to make my own decisions, even when you disagree?

On the parents' part, there's genuine fear for their daughter's spiritual and emotional future. The subject isn't just academic or theological; there's a vast emotional contrast between discussing this with a friend and talking it over with a beloved child.

Sometimes the context of the discussion is filled with legitimate concerns, and in fairness, it can also include less-than-healthy ones. I've seen, for instance, the desire to retain parental influence, even control, become the primary issue. Then the debate isn't just about sexuality—it's about who's in charge.

History, too, plays into the context. If a daughter's relationship with Mom and Dad has been reasonably good, that increases the likelihood of a healthy discussion. But an already less-than-ideal dynamic will add emotional hurdles to the factual and perceptual obstacles.

I remember clearly my conversations with Traditionalists when I was a Revisionist. If over the years we'd had a positive relationship, then we felt deep sadness that we were now divided, strong desire to understand each other, mutual respect due to our shared experiences, and hope for goodwill even as we disagreed. But if we'd had a negative history, I was far more defensive, aggressive, even dismissive. Not so much because of our contrary viewpoints, but because we hadn't gotten along anyway. Personal history made all the difference.

So Where Does That Leave Us?

Most of these chapters will deal with content (what to say and how), but knowing the context of our conversation can help us anticipate problems, adjust our approach, and stay sensitive to the perceptions and feelings of the other.

When Jesus waded into a dialogue laden with negative context, His high priority was for the Samaritan woman to know Him, and thereby to know life. That desire kept the conversation focused on three main points:

1. *Who He was:* He spoke plainly about His divinity and made no bones about His right to the title *Messiah* (John 4:25–26).
2. *Where she was:* He accurately described her sexual history, neither condoning nor harping on it (4:16–18).
3. *What He offered:* He offered *Himself,* not just as a way to abandon her lifestyle, but as the answer to her deepest temporal and eternal needs (4:10–14).

Ultimately, our hope is to likewise see something happen between our gay or pro-gay friend and God Himself. All ethical arguments, then, should lead back to the person of Jesus Christ, clarifying who He is, His awareness of where our friend is, and what He offers.

Wading through the complicated, emotionally packed context of our conversations with homosexual people, we could do far worse than to follow Jesus's lead.

2

TO WHOM AM I SPEAKING?

I have become all things to all men, that I might by all means save some.

—1 Corinthians 9:22

The gain of even "some" is worth the expenditure of "all means."

—*Jamieson-Fausset-Brown Bible Commentary*

A good steward studies the truth he's been entrusted with; a good ambassador studies the people to whom he's sent.

When we speak about homosexuality, we're speaking to a culture with whom we're no longer necessarily on the same page. So it's in our interest to develop an understanding, not only of our topic, but of the people with whom we're likely to discuss it. That will include five groups we'll address in this chapter: *militants*, *mainstream*, *millennials*, *Revisionists*, and *friends and family* members. Not everyone is going to fit neatly into one of these, but we should recognize them as significant populations.

If we better understand some of these groups' concerns, their tensions with us, and appropriate conversational goals with them, we'll better fulfill our roles as ambassadors.

I should also stress that ambassadors have a primary responsibility to the one who sent them, and a secondary responsibility to those to whom they're sent. Our primary goal is pleasing the Sender, honoring Him by handling His truths and representing Him well. But along with pleasing Him, we long to reach the people to whom we're sent.

Paul said as much to the Romans when he bared his feelings about his fellow Hebrews: "I have great sorrow and continual grief in my heart. For I could wish that I myself were accursed from Christ for my brethren" (Rom. 9:2–3). That's the longing of an ambassador who cares deeply about the people he hopes to reach. But this same ambassador clarified that, given the choice between the approval of people versus the approval of the Sender, there's no contest: "Do I seek to please men? For if I still pleased men, I would not be a bondservant of Christ" (Gal. 1:10).

We care, as Paul did, for the people, and we hope to see them reached. But the response can be explosive. We all know that this hot topic sometimes generates outright hostility, which is unfairly but squarely directed at us. So we need to avoid the error of interpreting a bad response as bad stewardship on our part.

When we answer to our Sender, it won't be for how well we were received. It will be for how faithfully we represented Him.

Evangelizing, Discipling, Reasoning

Depending on the other person's spiritual status, we'll have the goal of evangelizing an unbeliever, discipling a believer in error, or simply reasoning with someone about our differing views. Keep these goals in mind, because the end goal should steer the conversation.

For example, if I'm talking about sexuality with a non-Christian, my hope—therefore, my goal—is her conversion. So I'll try to use the sexual issue to bring the conversation to ideas about how we determine right or wrong, whether or not we were created, and if so, how we can know our Creator. That leads to discussions about the validity of the Bible, which in turn lead to the claims and promises of Christ. The end goal steers the discussion.

As stewards and ambassadors with these goals, let's consider people with whom we're likely to discuss homosexuality.

Militants

Militants, whether homosexual or heterosexual, are convinced not only that homosexuality is normal, but that those who oppose it are contemptible and should be converted or silenced. This contrasts with the many homosexuals who don't view us as enemies.

Militants are angry, a fact about which they make no bones and feel justified. For that reason they're prone to bullying, though they'll seldom admit it. Instead they view their attitude and tactics as righteous responses to injustice, something akin to Dr. King's civil rights resistance.

Gay journalist and icon Dan Savage, for example, when guest speaking at a student journalism conference, mocked the Bible and believers by referring to the "bull— in the Bible about homosexuality" and calling Christians who walked out on his profanity-laced tirade "pansy-a—ed."[1]

In a similar tone, activist Larry Kramer referred proudly to his group ACT UP's invasion of a Catholic mass in New York City, in which demonstrators stopped the service by jumping into the aisles and screaming. "And suddenly," Kramer said, "we were no longer limp-wristed fairies. We were men in black boots and black jeans and tough, and that became our image. And it made us, I think. And people were suddenly afraid of us. . . . It's a good feeling."[2]

The militant's anger may well have its genesis in early bullying the bully himself suffered, which he is now taking out on perceived enemies. Or it could come from a belief that conservative Christians belong to the same class as Nazis and the KKK. Regardless, he doesn't "agree to disagree" with us. He believes there's no room for our viewpoint in a decent society.

Conversations with militants tend to be marked by tension, largely because they won't allow us to find much common ground with them. But our primary points of disagreement are over the morality of homosexuality, the rights Christians should or should not have for expressing their views, and the question of whether the traditional viewpoint can really be equated with racism and hatred.

Tensions notwithstanding, gay and pro-gay militants aren't necessarily hateful, just thoroughly convinced. I've found it helpful to listen carefully to their charges against us, then admit when I agree with them. They'll complain about what Christians have said or done that they find hateful. If possible, I'll validate their legitimate complaints, then bring up the broader issue of Christ Himself, rather than Christians. I also try to reason with them about the difference between prejudice (a belief in the superiority of one person over another) and standards (a belief in the superiority of some behaviors over others).

Granted, the unreasonable, aggressive tone some militants take can limit the chance of reasonable dialogue. Worse, it can tempt you to hostility, a temptation with which believers over the centuries have had to cope.

Look again at Acts and you'll find a record of militant tactics thrown at the early apostles by people who wanted to silence or even kill them. To their credit the Christians withdrew as needed or confronted as led, but never allowed personal hostility to poison them or their service. There's a lot we can learn from them.

Mainstream

Most same-sex-attracted people and their supporters could be described as *mainstream*, fellow humans and citizens with whom we have more in common than differences. And, per Jesus, they're our neighbors, whom we're to love and serve.

Some generalizations may be accurate. People who identify as lesbian or gay tend to be politically liberal, though gay conservatives certainly exist. They will probably have had more sexual partners than the average heterosexual, though again, some are virgins and will remain so, and others are either celibate or very moderate sexually. And most will have had more relationships (whether legal marriages or live-in pairings) than most heterosexuals.

Their childhood experiences are often more problematic than those of heterosexuals, usually because of early gender nonconformity, and in many cases they've kept major parts of their lives secret, depending on where, when, and how they were raised.

More important than generalities, though, is the fact all homosexuals are loved, valued, and desired by God. They're our co-workers, friends, or schoolmates, people with whom we interact for any number of reasons. And since homosexuality has gained broad acceptance, they're more likely than ever to be "out of the closet." But that doesn't necessarily make them hostile to us. Many homosexual people are in fact people of goodwill, likable, and fair. For every Larry Kramer or Dan Savage, there's a homosexual person who's decent and reasonable.

Of course, a mainstream person may feel strongly about this subject, having wrestled with it personally and come to a point of accepting his sexuality. We commonly hear, "I finally am at peace with this. I tried denying it, and life was miserable. So don't try putting me back in that closet!" But that hardly makes them hostile.

Nor does it make them unreachable. We should show them respect and kindness and offer friendship as opportunity allows. In that context you will probably come across chances to share the gospel and to reason with them, since ongoing relationships can lead to discussions about sexual, political, and spiritual issues. Chapters 4–13 will cover subjects likely to arise in those discussions.

Millennials

It's a mistake to presume too much about someone based on a generational label, like *boomer*, *Gen X*, and the rest. Human nature and human need haven't changed so much over the centuries, so classifications of any age-group can overgeneralize.

Still, one significant detail about *millennials* (those born between 1978 and 2000, according to most sources) is that they're the first generation to come of age in a largely prohomosexual culture. They warrant special mention here.

Assumptions about sexuality on which prior generations of Americans were raised haven't been so prevalent in their lives, so the disconnect between traditional biblical teaching and their cultural surroundings is larger than any other US generation has experienced.

They've grown up viewing openly gay, sympathetically portrayed television characters. They've witnessed countless athletes, politicians, comedians, religious leaders, actors, and musicians declare themselves "out and proud." Their sense of justice has developed under the influence of a media openly aligned with the gay rights movement, an education system committed to teaching them homosexuality is normal, and an entertainment industry devoted to pro-gay causes.

Is anyone really surprised, then, that 69 percent of millennials surveyed express support for same-sex marriage, and that nearly a quarter report leaving the church of their upbringing because of its "negative" teachings about homosexuality?[3] Millennials, it seems, often and sincerely view Traditionalist boomers like me the way I grew up viewing segregationists of the 1960s. This is not to say millennials share the militant's hostility toward Traditionalists. Rather, they seem to shrug and say, "So someone's gay! I don't see what the big deal is." Raised with different structural presumptions, they've come to different conclusions as well.

Non-Christian millennials will almost certainly view homosexuality as normal. Christian millennials might believe the same, depending on how they view Scripture. Some who are more "progressive" will claim respect for the Bible but not belief that it's authoritative in all areas. Those holding a higher view of Scripture may believe homosexuality is wrong but are not comfortable with the way prior generations of Christians have handled it.

Reasoning is often a vital part of evangelism and discipleship, one which seems tailor-made for dialogue with them. Your story about your relationship with God, with principles you've drawn from that relationship about right and wrong, is unique to you. You should share it, as you also listen carefully to similar stories from the millennial. That forms a basis for exchange, based on mutual respect and willingness to consider alternative options, both of which this group values.

Christian Revisionists

Whether openly homosexual or heterosexual but "gay affirming," Christian Revisionists identify themselves as Christians who believe the Bible is authoritative, and that it's been broadly misunderstood on this matter. (This is in contrast to Revisionists in general, who hold a prohomosexual viewpoint but not a religious one. For brevity's sake, in the coming chapters we'll use "Revisionists" as a word describing either.) They promote revised interpretations of scriptural references to homosexuality, saying those verses have been mistranslated or misinterpreted. The authority of the Bible has not changed, nor has God, they say. But our understanding of both needs to change.

Since these are professing believers, dialogue with them is less evangelistic and more discipleship- and apologetics-oriented, based on our common regard for Scripture. As a discipleship issue, Revisionism and the "gay Christian" phenomenon need to be carefully examined and responded to. Because ultimately they either indicate (as Revisionists believe) a seismic reformation long overdue or (as Traditionalists believe) a gargantuan doctrinal and moral error.

Both parties agree that the subject is vital, permanently impacting church policies for membership, discipline, and doctrine on a global scale. So this book will give it the attention it requires.

Friends and Family Members

When homosexuality hits home, the debate taps into our primary feelings and fears, complicating the discussion. Someone you love, whether friend or family member, may fall into the militant, mainstream, millennial, or Revisionist categories, but the fact that you're bonded to that person adds a new layer to the dialogue. The two of you share history and emotional connection, and sometimes it's someone whose sexuality directly and hugely affects you. If a son or daughter comes out to you, or a spouse, or even a close friend, you're likely to deal with a whole range of emotions attached to the new knowledge. You must deal with new assumptions, new ways of relating.

Whole books have been written on this (including my own *When Homosexuality Hits Home*[4]), but for our purposes, when focusing on dialogue challenges, remember a couple of points:

First, you may need to address and even correct the context of your relationship before a productive dialogue on homosexuality can happen. With a spouse, for example, you clearly need to arrive at agreed-upon terms and expectations. With a friend with whom you've had a rocky relationship, you'll need to establish a peace before the let's-talk-about-sexuality part. Context is always trickier when there's history, and history is always trickier when it includes family intimacy.

And second, you may need a trusted friend, counselor, or pastor to help you sort through your feelings and difficulties with this. Parents, for example, experience emotions often associated with grief when a son or daughter comes out to them, because their assumptions about their loved one are having to die. So don't shy away from getting necessary support during what may be a literal grieving process.

Now that we understand something about the context of our conversation and with whom we're trying to communicate, let's examine a few guidelines for conducting a conversation that has the best chance of achieving God's goals for the dialogue.

3

RULES OF ENGAGEMENT

The two words "information" and "communication" are often
used interchangeably, but they signify quite different things.
Information is giving out; communication is getting through.

—Sydney Harris

I'm fascinated and delighted with the concept of God enlisting
humanity to be part of His work.

It would all go more smoothly if He didn't, you know. If angels
preached the gospel instead of people, there'd be more conversions, fewer mishaps, no scandals. But imperfect humanity gets
the honor of participating in God's purposes, so the gospel is
committed to men. Amazing.

But I think I get it. When my youngest son was a toddler, he
used to join me in the backyard while I mowed the lawn, and
nothing would satisfy him but to help me. Obviously, I steered
and did the heavy lifting with a wide grip on the handlebars,
while he kept a narrow grip in the middle, and together we
pushed and made our way around the yard.

It took about four times longer than if I'd done it alone, and I'd certainly have done it better. But my boy was taking part in my work, and the father-son alignment, accomplishing the task however imperfectly, was a joy to both.

God commissions truth to us toddlers, who wander about the yard, pushing with a narrow grip, doing our part. We speak the Word, then He, doing the heavy lifting with a wide grip, backs our efforts by convicting hearts, imparting faith, or removing blinders, finalizing the job. We and God unite in cooperative effort, not because He needs us, but because the Father-child alignment, accomplishing the task imperfectly, is a joy to both.

So He makes us stewards of truth, first to learn it, then to live it, and finally, to express it. God is seeking to communicate truth, to save people in error from eternal death or temporal ruin. That's our Father's business, the lawn mower we latch on to.

So truths should be expressed by His stewards and heard by people who'll then be objects of the Holy Spirit's heavy lifting. As a steward, you're entrusted with eternal truths and expected to handle them well. And as an ambassador, you represent your Sender to those with whom He wants to make peace. How do you best represent Him? Let's review *seven rules of engagement when speaking of homosexuality.*

Rule 1: Speak Clearly

Speak *clearly* when expressing God-ordained standards and definitions, neither of which are useful if not clear. Vague moral standards can't be met. Nebulous definitions mean little. If you're nonspecific when you speak, your listeners will assume what you're saying is also non-important.

Paul rhetorically asked the Corinthians, "If the trumpet makes an uncertain sound, who will prepare for battle?" (1 Cor. 14:8). You should be making three things clear when you discuss homosexuality: *where* you stand, the *importance* of the issue, and your belief that your stand is both *fair* and *loving*. If you aren't convinced of these, your uncertainty will be obvious, so please be sure to settle your stance in your own mind first.

I say all this because an alarming number of Christians, and even Christian leaders, seem to think there's virtue in being vague. Some refuse to take a clear position on homosexuality for fear of the fallout; some are actually proud of being coy about their stance, as though it's godly to grin and "keep 'em guessing." Others think it intellectually superior to be ambiguous rather than settled, as if robust conviction is the realm of the Neanderthal.

Let's shed any false notions that God is unsure what's right or wrong, or that clear positions are somehow too simplistic. Clarity is a biblical essential, a trademark of responsible Christian communication. Never apologize for speaking to be understood.

Rule 2: Speak Appropriately

The right thing spoken at the wrong time makes a big mess. When Solomon said, "A word fitly spoken is like apples of gold in settings of silver" (Prov. 25:11), his word "fitly" denoted "circumstance, condition, and timeliness" in Hebrew. In other words, watch your timing and mind your priorities.

Now if someone says, "Where do you stand on same-sex marriage?" the timing's obviously right to speak plainly, and I never advise ducking a direct question. But usually, before discussing homosexuality, you'll consider how well you know the person, the best timing for the conversation, and the priority issues in your approach to that person. Ambassadors retain a good sense of when to speak and what to focus on.

Rule 3: Speak Empathically

Empathy is important because people need to believe you can relate. Empathy communicates the ability to understand and share another's feelings. And if you consider your own experience, I think you'll find plenty of material to draw on. You know what it's like to feel different from others in some way. You know what it's like to have unwanted feelings. You know what it's like to keep a secret, to wish the Bible said something other than what it does, to be angry, to consider indulging or rejecting a vital part of yourself. You can relate to all that.

So congratulations. You have what it takes to empathize, maybe not completely but largely, with a homosexual person. Draw on your own experiences to communicate empathy, and that alone will have impact.

Rule 4: Concede What's True

Attorneys argue with an eye toward winning the case, not arriving at the truth. In courtroom battles, what's true is secondary to what works, so conceding a point is rarely an option.

But when you're speaking of homosexuality with someone who's pro-gay or openly homosexual, you're speaking as a friend and a servant, so scoring points means less than honest communication. Sometimes we don't like the hard truths that emerge in discussions, but if they're true, they should be acknowledged, not refuted. We can't, after all, ask a homosexual person to consider inconvenient truths if we're unwilling to do the same.

There's plenty of inconvenient truth to go around, and while we shouldn't apologize for taking a biblical stand, I've heard enough irresponsible, inaccurate, contemptuous words from Christians hurled at homosexuals, both in front of the pulpit and behind it, to know that many complaints we hear about believers are true.

Some points worth conceding, then, are these:

- "Lots of Christians have said hateful things about gays."
- "Christians have been wrong in the past."
- "We don't always know what causes homosexuality."
- "Some ministers have given lousy advice to gay parishioners."
- "Lots of Christians have supported antigay laws just because they were antigay, without even thinking them through!"
- "Plenty of Christians used to say AIDS was God's judgment on gays."
- "Lots of Christians are more upset about homosexuality than they are about adultery or fornication, even though those are condemned in the Bible."

If something's true, like it or not, concede it. As stewards of truth, we won't duck the very thing we say we value.

Rule 5: Consider What's Possible

In 1991, when a handful of studies were released suggesting homosexuality may be inborn, I was struck by the number of Christians who insisted there could be no biological or genetic component to this whatsoever. Many of us seemed to think that admitting inborn characteristics might play into this was akin to waving a white flag.

But "it's possible" is a legitimate response to questions about the origins of homosexuality, without having to veer outside biblical guidelines. It's also a legitimate response to statements like "I know gay couples who've been together for decades," "God used a gay person to share the gospel with me," or "Lots of my gay friends are happier than my Christian friends." All of that is possible; none of it invalidates the Traditionalist position. A reasonable person considers an argument's possibility, admitting it may be true, while explaining why it doesn't alter his basic positions.

Rule 6: Watch the Apologies

Christian leaders have made a number of public apologies to the gay community over the past few years, and while they're no doubt well intended, the message they send has become confusing. Many of these apologies don't clarify what sins are being confessed. To simply say, "We've been unloving," without qualifying whether "unloving" means rude or insulting, or whether it means speaking words that someone preferred not to hear, creates more problems than it solves.

Now, anyone who's been rude, uncaring, unfair, or even hateful has lots to apologize for. But while some believers have been all of those, is it really fair to say *all* believers have, and therefore to apologize for the entire body of Christ?

If you've been wrong, own it. If you feel compassion over something a homosexual friend or loved one experienced at the hands of a Christian, saying you're sorry that happened, in the sense that you empathize, is completely appropriate. That's not an apology; that's a gesture of concern. But remember, we answer to God for our own sins; we're in no position to take responsibility for someone else's.

Rule 7: Recognize and Point Out Diversions

A diversion is a strategy to distract the focus from the main point and park attention on a secondary issue. When a Traditionalist says, "Same-sex relations fall short of what God designed," and a Revisionist says, "But gays can't change," that's a diversion from the sin issue to the outcome issue.

Point out the diversion—"We're not talking about whether or not it's changeable; we're talking about whether or not it's right"—and refocus on your original point. (For example, "Whether or not you experience temptation toward a behavior doesn't settle whether the behavior is right or wrong.")

Other common diversions include

- "Your position causes gays to commit suicide."
- "Segregationists said the same things about African Americans that you're saying about gays."
- "Look how many Christians get divorced!"

All of those are legitimate points to pursue, but they're diversionary tactics when used to distract from the issue you've agreed to discuss. When diversions are thrown at you, it's helpful to answer, "That's a good point but not the one we're discussing. Let's come back to that, but let me finish this point first."

Having established some guidelines for discussion, let's now take a look at some of the issues we're likely to be discussing.

4

BORN GAY?

DNA is not the heart's destiny; the genetic lottery may determine the cards in your deck, but experience deals the hand you can play.

—Thomas Lewis

Theories on the origins of homosexuality tend to fall into one of four categories: The *inborn theory* (homosexuals are born that way), the *developmental theory* (family dynamics and early experiences cause homosexuality), the *spiritual theory* (homosexuality is caused by demonic forces), and the *behavioral choice theory* (homosexuals choose to be that way).

The inborn theory remains the most popular, widely accepted in the general culture, and the developmental theory, though controversial, still enjoys some support among conservatives. But since the inborn theory is widely held, it's the one most likely to arise in conversations on homosexuality, so it warrants our attention.

Between fall 1991 and summer 1992, a handful of studies were released suggesting homosexuality may have a genetic or biological component.[1] The reactions, both favorable and condemning, were extraordinary. The media emblazoned the research in headlines suggesting "born gay" was now a proven fact, though the researchers themselves categorically denied they'd proven any such thing. Gay advocates rushed in to underscore the implications, insisting that if homosexuality was inborn, it couldn't be sinful or abnormal. And conservatives scrambled to discredit the research, finding a number of genuine flaws in methodology and interpretation.[2]

Two broad messages were going out, and they've echoed through the culture ever since: Homosexuality is inborn, and if homosexuality is inborn, it must be legitimized.

Countless other studies over the past twenty-five years have claimed similar findings. Almost yearly, another headline proclaims that the most convincing proof to date is now in: People are born gay. And the dynamic between Revisionists and Traditionalists has stayed essentially the same. Many Revisionists say, "Here's the proof: Gay is inborn, not chosen, so gay is OK," with many Traditionalists rebutting, "Here's where your proof is lacking: Gay is still a choice, and not OK."

Both are wrong, primarily in their oversimplification of both the research and its implications. Studies released to date have never claimed to prove conclusively that homosexuality is inborn, so it's a misinterpretation to say they do. It's likewise inaccurate to say that if homosexuality is not inborn, it must therefore be a simple choice. A Traditionalist can maintain a biblical view of homosexuality while recognizing the possibility that some inborn elements may contribute to it.

Traditional Position

The Bible condemns homosexual acts and describes homosexual desires as "vile" (Rom. 1:26), without explaining specifically what causes them. Inborn elements could be contributors, so the inborn theory could have merit. That would not, in itself, legitimize homosexuality.

REVISIONIST ARGUMENT 1

Homosexuality has been proven to be inborn.

"The only people who don't think you're born gay are Pat Robertson and Anne Heche," quipped comedian Bill Maher,[3] expressing what many believe today: "Everyone knows gays are born that way. It's common knowledge. The debate's over."

FIRST RESPONSE: **Universal consensus doesn't exist among experts.**

Repeat something often enough and people will assume it's true without examining it. This holds true especially if the something being repeated is a simplistic sound bite. We saw this decades ago when it was widely assumed that 10 percent of the population was homosexual. That "common knowledge" existed because it was repeated so often, not because it was ever proven. In fact, it's been soundly debunked.

No matter. If people hear something often enough, especially if it comes from experts, they're inclined to believe it because, after all, how could so many experts be wrong?

Yet the American Psychological Association, an open champion of gay rights, states plainly,

There is no consensus among scientists about the exact reasons that an individual develops a heterosexual, bisexual, gay or lesbian orientation. Although much research has examined the possible genetic, hormonal, developmental, social and cultural influences on sexual orientation, no findings have emerged that permit scientists to conclude that sexual orientation is determined by any particular factor or factors. Many think that nature and nurture both play complex roles; most people experience little or no sense of choice about their sexual orientation.[4]

Geneticist Sven Bocklandt of the David Geffen School of Medicine at UCLA makes a similar observation: "There is no single 'gay gene'—no single switch for sexual orientation. Instead, there are probably a handful of genes that work in ways as yet unexplained."[5] Lesbian life expert Kathy Belge comments, "Despite social science and biological research, it is still not known what causes someone to be gay, lesbian, bisexual or straight."[6] And Dr. Anne Fausto-Sterling, chair of science and technology studies at Brown University, dismisses the idea of a "gay gene" or singular inborn cause for homosexuality: "Traits and feelings are processes, not things."[7]

There is currently no uniform consensus among scientists and mental health experts regarding the origins of homosexuality. While most agree that homosexuality is normal and, in fact, most support the goals of the gay rights movement, their own jury still seems to be out on the question of whether homosexuality is inborn or acquired.

SECOND RESPONSE: **Homosexuality may be created by a constellation of influences, not all of them identifiable.**

Homosexuality itself may not be inborn, but genetic characteristics could make a person more susceptible to it later in life.

Researchers William Byne and Bruce Parsons explain, "For example, if a gene influenced some factor, such as temperament, in a manner that would increase the probability of homosexual development in a particular environment, that gene could be called a gene for homosexuality with reduced penetrance."[8]

Cornell University professor and respected social psychologist Daryl J. Bem seems to agree when he writes,

> Biological factors influence sexual orientation only indirectly, by intervening earlier in the chain of events to determine a child's temperaments and subsequent activity preferences. . . . Correlation between a biological factor and sexual orientation is more plausibly attributed to its influence in early childhood than to a direct link with sexual orientation.[9]

I have long believed there's merit to the developmental theory, having seen similar family dynamics in the lives of hundreds of homosexual men with whom I've worked for nearly thirty years. I see patterns of similar interactions with both father and mother, and similar relational issues and situations with peers. The profiles are often the same.

Yet many lifelong heterosexual men with the same backgrounds and profiles have never felt same-sex attraction. Perhaps, then, there are inborn personality traits that make a person more susceptible to homosexuality if other postnatal, environmental circumstances occur. That hardly means one is born homosexual, but it could mean one is born with a susceptibility to it if certain family or childhood factors come into play.

Still, if homosexuality has not been proven to be inborn, and since experts don't agree that it's an inherited trait, and since a number of influences (not all of them identifiable) probably combine to create it, it's safe to say that the inborn argument is an oversimplification.

REVISIONIST ARGUMENT 2

Since homosexuality has been proven to be
inborn, it must therefore be normal.

Dr. Richard Pillard, one of the researchers whose work was reported in 1991 to indicate an inborn component of homosexuality, said he hoped his findings would cause homosexual people to realize, "This is not a fault. This is not your fault."[10] That summarizes what many people believe: If something is inborn, there must be nothing wrong with it.

RESPONSE: **A number of unhealthy tendencies seem to be inborn, so inborn doesn't necessarily mean "healthy" or "normal."**

In May 2004 the *Journal of Neuroscience* released findings linking a gene to alcohol addiction.[11]

Two years earlier Dr. Redford Williams of Duke University said evidence of an "anger gene" had been found.[12]

A "depression gene" was suggested in 2011 after an analysis of fifty-four studies indicated its existence.[13]

And capping it off, we're now considering a gene for— drum roll—that nasty tendency men have toward a wandering eye. Dr. Richard Friedman reported in May 2015 that it may not be their fault after all, because "Infidelity Lurks in Your Genes."[14]

It may be true that all these conditions are inborn. Clearly, though, we don't presume a condition is healthy because of its inborn status. Otherwise we could excuse alcoholism, depression, anger problems, and infidelity all as "healthy," since they, too, may be inborn.

REVISIONIST ARGUMENT 3

Since homosexuality has been proven to be
inborn, it must have been intended by God.

Christian artist Ray Boltz, best known for the popular song "Thank You (for Giving to the Lord)," has declared himself gay and Christian: "If this is the way God made me, then this is the way I'm going to live. It's not like God made me this way and he'll send me to hell if I am who he created me to be."[15]

His sentiments are common, going something like this: "If I was born gay, I was born gay by design, so my Creator intends me to be gay."

RESPONSE: **We are a fallen race, imperfect physically, emotionally, spiritually. Inborn does not mean "God-ordained."**

When God pronounced what's commonly called the curse in Eden after Adam's sin, He told Adam and Eve that they'd now experience a number of spiritual, relational, and physical consequences He never intended. They would physically decay and die; they would have power struggles between themselves; the environment would become adversarial. In short, the human experience would now be marked with physical, emotional, and spiritual conflict that wasn't part of God's Plan A (Gen. 3).

Sin affects us physically as well as spiritually, so we could never with biblical integrity defend a tendency as "God-given," even if it's inborn. The human race is subject to physical imperfections, some even showing up at birth, along with a spiritually dead sinful nature.

David said, "Behold, I was brought forth in iniquity, and in sin my mother conceived me" (Ps. 51:5), and in Psalm 58:3 he added, "The wicked are estranged from the womb; they go astray as soon as they are born, speaking lies." Anyone who has raised children will tell you that they lie, act selfish, and become defiant with no coaching from anyone. They, like all of us, are natural-born sinners, having inherited the sin nature from their first father, Adam, which has affected them on every level.

So "born this way" cannot justify anything. It only tells us what we already know: We're born in sin; some sinful tendencies may be influenced by inborn physical characteristics; and above all, we must be born again.

Unfair? Maybe. Justification? No.

We generally don't determine whether something's right or wrong by what caused it but rather by the thing itself. So we can allow for the possibility that homosexual tendencies may either be inborn or influenced by inborn traits, though we also recognize research can be publicized as conclusive and later found to be something less. *Psychology Today* noted this trend: "Many discoveries loudly touted to the public have been quietly refuted by further research."[16]

Regardless, whether a tendency is pre- or postnatal, if it inclines us toward what God never intended, then it remains sinful, whatever its genesis.

Ten Talking Points about the Inborn Theory

1. It has not been conclusively proven (as of 2015) that homosexuality is inborn. This is often claimed and commonly believed, but not conclusively proven.

2. Numerous studies over the past twenty-five years have suggested a biological or genetic component to homosexuality, and each study should be considered on its own merit.

3. It's entirely possible there are inborn elements contributing to homosexuality, which most likely develop from a combination of influences, some inborn, some environmental.

4. Experts are by no means uniform in their belief about what causes homosexuality.

5. Research has too often been politicized, in the ways it's both conducted and interpreted, to promote an agenda rather than reach objective conclusions.

6. Many unhealthy conditions—addiction, violence, even promiscuous tendencies—may be inborn. But none of these behaviors are thereby legitimized.

7. If everything inborn is good, how do we account for birth defects?

8. "Fallen nature" is a biblical concept recognizing we are born in sin, imperfect physically, psychologically, and spiritually. So a biblical worldview allows for the possibility of inborn sinful tendencies.

9. The fact that many homosexual people believe their orientation is inborn speaks to how deeply that orientation is ingrained.

10. When calling people to take up their crosses, we should remember that for them it may mean saying no to some of their most deeply ingrained intimacy desires, leaving them facing the possibility of lifelong celibacy. This may be the right choice, but believers should recognize its enormity when they call the homosexual to repentance.

5

THE "CHANGE" CONTROVERSY

So maybe my nature does draw me to you, that don't mean I
have to go with it. I can take hold of myself and I can say yes to
some things and no to other things that are gonna ruin everything! I can do that. Otherwise, you know, what, what good is
this stupid life that God gave us?

—from the film *Moonstruck*

On June 20, 2013, the executive director of Exodus International, widely considered the largest organization promoting
the idea that homosexuality can be overcome, dropped a bomb
at its annual conference, issuing an open apology to the gay
community. He expressed regret over having told gays they
could change: "I am sorry that some of you spent years working through the shame and guilt you felt when your attractions
didn't change. I am sorry we promoted sexual orientation change
efforts and reparative theories about sexual orientation that
stigmatized parents."[1]

He then announced that Exodus, for nearly forty years considered the premiere international Christian resource promoting freedom from homosexuality, was closing.

Picked up by the media as a death knell to the "ex-gay movement," this was in fact one of many incremental moves toward a widespread rejection of the idea that homosexuality is changeable.

The mental health industry has challenged the idea for years. The American Academy of Pediatrics, the American Counseling Association, the American Psychiatric Association, the American Psychological Association (APA), the American School Counselor Association, and the National Association of Social Workers have all officially denounced any therapeutic efforts aimed at changing a person's sexual orientation.[2]

Additionally, state laws banning *reparative therapy* for minors have, as of this writing, been passed in California, New Jersey, Oregon, Illinois, and the District of Columbia, and bills have been introduced to make the treatment illegal for anyone of any age.

Can homosexual desires be changed to heterosexual ones, or eradicated, or both? Most commonly associated with a yes answer are Exodus (the Exodus Global Alliance still operates worldwide), the National Association for Research and Therapy for Homosexuality (NARTH, an international network of clinicians), the Restored Hope Network (an American referral network of Christian ministries), and the Hope for Wholeness Network (another Christian network).

Ministries, psychologists, or therapists offering help to repentant homosexuals are often described as doing "reparative therapy" or being "ex-gay ministries." Reparative therapy is a secular psychoanalytic approach to treating homosexuality, largely developed by psychologist Dr. Joseph Nicolosi, based on Freudian and neo-Freudian concepts. It has enjoyed popularity among Christians, conservative Jews, and Mormons.

Ex-gay ministries, in contrast, are usually not clinical, offering instead combinations of education, mentoring, and group support for people who experience unwanted same-sex attractions.

Reparative therapy has largely become a pejorative term, inaccurately applied to any ministry or counselor taking the Traditionalist view, even though true reparative therapy must be performed by a licensed mental health professional in a clinical environment and adhere to psychoanalytic theories. So references to Exodus or similar ministries doing reparative therapy are inaccurate.

Ex-gay, likewise, is commonly used as a slur, often associated with the phrase "pray the gay away." Christians who struggle with unwanted homosexuality usually avoid such labels, though some refer to themselves as having "unwanted SSA" (same-sex attractions), and fewer still refer to themselves as gay Christians.

For the Traditionalist, who believes homosexual desires are manifestations of fallen nature and that homosexual sex is a sin, whether or not those desires can be fully eradicated is not cut-and-dried. We can, after all, believe something to be wrong and repent, yet still be tempted toward it.

Meanwhile, our culture is settling firmly into the conviction "Once gay, always gay." Only a third of Americans consider homosexuality changeable, per a 2013 survey,[3] and those numbers will likely shrink, since approval of homosexuality raises skepticism about attempts to change it.

Is homosexuality curable? Are efforts to change good or damaging? And what should we make of claims that therapy to change homosexuality should be criminalized?

Traditional Position 1

The general Traditionalist position on change regarding sin of any sort is

1. Sinful acts can be stopped.
2. Temptations may stop, though usually not completely.
3. Temptations may and often do decrease in power.
4. Temptations, to whatever extent they remain, can be resisted and needn't define the individual.
5. If behavior, self-identification, relational patterns, and general spiritual and emotional well-being have increased, then the individual has changed.

Homosexual behavior is declared a sin five times in the Bible: Leviticus 18:22; 20:13; Romans 1:26–27; 1 Corinthians 6:9; 1 Timothy 1:10. Accordingly, like any other sin, it can be repented of (stopped), and the person need no longer be identified with it. Rather, he or she is a new creation in Christ (2 Cor. 5:17), whose posture toward old ways is summed up in Paul's assertion: "Such were some of you. But you were washed, you were sanctified, you were justified in the name of the Lord Jesus and by the Spirit of our God" (1 Cor. 6:11 ESV).

The renounced sin need not have power over the individual, who is free to choose not to repeat the behavior (Rom. 6:12–14). Yet temptation toward sin, or "sinful tendencies," is assumed per 1 John 1:8 and Galatians 5:17. The Bible never guarantees that renunciation of sin will prevent future temptation. But the individual is promised the ability to resist temptations that may come ("God is faithful, who will not allow you to be tempted beyond what you are able, but with the temptation will also make the way of escape, that you may be able to bear it," 1 Cor. 10:13).

We assume that repentance from homosexual behavior follows the pattern of repentance from other sins. It can be stopped, the individual no longer needing to identify with it by adopting labels like "gay," "lesbian," "gay Christian," or "LGBT," but rather "washed" and "sanctified."

When an individual turns from sins—in this case homosexual acts—finding freedom from their power over him, in both behavior and identity the individual has "changed."

Yet homosexual temptations, or "tendencies," are likely to continue to some extent. Each experience is unique, and people report differing degrees of temptation's severity, but God offers every Christian the power to resist. So the Bible promises change of identity and behavior, as well as the power to resist temptation, thereby overcoming sin's hold.

REVISIONIST ARGUMENT 1

Immutability: Sexual orientation cannot be changed.

The Revisionist conviction is that, if you're attracted to the same sex, you'll always be gay in your orientation, therefore change is impossible. Once gay, always gay.

FIRST RESPONSE: **There's no solid consensus on what the term** *sexual orientation* **even means.**

You'd think it just meant "what turns you on," but you'd be wrong. According to the American Psychological Association, sexual orientation refers to "an enduring emotional, romantic, or sexual attraction toward men, toward women, or toward both."[4] By that definition one could be *sexually* attracted to the same sex, *emotionally* attracted to the opposite sex, and thereby a little of both orientations.

The *Merriam-Webster Medical Dictionary* definition of *sexual orientation* is more succinct: "the inclination of an individual with respect to heterosexual, homosexual, and bisexual behavior."[5] Yet this, too, invites confusion. Many people attracted to the same sex are not inclined toward same-sex behavior. They've never considered it, finding it contradictory to their worldview. So are they heterosexual because of behavior, in spite of their attractions?

The Human Rights Campaign, one of the world's largest pro-gay lobbying organizations, defines sexual orientation as "an inherent or immutable enduring emotional, romantic or sexual attraction to other people."[6] But one who has an enduring *emotional* attraction to someone of the same sex, without any *sexual* attraction, could hardly be called "homosexual," since *sexual* isn't part of the equation. It could be called deep love, friendship, or even "bromance." But *sexual orientation* wouldn't apply.

The American Psychological Association also recognizes that the strict "gay" or "straight" categories don't always work: "While these categories continue to be widely used, research has suggested that sexual orientation does not always appear in such definable categories and instead occurs on a continuum."[7]

Writing for *The Federalist* on the difficulty of defining *sexual orientation*, Dr. Glenn Stanton of Focus on the Family highlighted comments from Dr. Randall Sell, assistant professor at the Joseph L. Mailman School of Public Health at Columbia: "At present it is clear that researchers are confused as to what they are studying when they assess sexual orientation in their research."[8] Which led professor Ann Tweedy of the Hamline University School of Law to contend that "individuals should be able to define their own sexual orientation."[9] Dr. Stanton notes that "no small number of LGBT theorists wholly agree."[10]

If experts don't agree on what sexual orientation is, and if many are saying it should mean whatever you want it to mean, then the term becomes meaningless. A Traditionalist rejecting homosexuality could say, "My orientation's heterosexual because I say it is." Conversely, a heterosexual wanting to "marry" his male friend only for insurance benefits could say, "My orientation's gay because I say it is."

How, then, can we say sexual orientation cannot change when we haven't even determined what it is?

SECOND RESPONSE: **The argument presumes an either/or definition of change not applied to other treatment approaches.**

Alcoholism and addiction are unquestionably treatable, though treatment doesn't claim to eradicate cravings. Yet no one's suggesting that if the patient still craves the drug, then treatment was ineffective, much less damaging. Nor is anyone suggesting the patient who stopped the behavior, no matter what else he feels, didn't change.

The American Psychiatric Association promises: "People can recover from addiction. Effective treatments are available."[11] Yet the American Psychological Association plainly says the patient may have relapses and return to drinking.[12] AddictionRecovery .net describes addiction as a "lifelong condition,"[13] WebMD says most experts believe feelings of pedophilia (sexual attraction to children) are incurable and can only be managed,[14] and the University of Pennsylvania Health System views addicts as people needing "lifelong treatment."[15]

Is anybody going to say treatments for drug abuse, pedophilia, or alcoholism shouldn't be offered because they're "merely" support and management tools rather than "cures"? Or that patients going sober don't significantly change in multiple ways as a result? Is it meaningless when an addict's cravings for a drug or behavior diminish with time and continued abstention?

If the answers are all no, and if experts call helping an individual abstain from unwanted behavior "recovery," then why can't a reparative therapist say the same?

THIRD RESPONSE: **If something's unchangeable, that hardly makes it acceptable.**

Prohomosexual apologists often argue that if homosexuality is inborn or immutable, then it must be legitimized (see chap. 4).

Does that thinking apply to alcoholism, drug addiction, gambling addictions, chronic depression, sexual addiction, or pedophilia? The rightness or wrongness of a thing is not determined by its changeableness. Some tendencies may never change, or may never change completely. That doesn't justify giving in to them. And if therapy cannot erase them, that doesn't discredit therapy.

REVISIONIST ARGUMENT 2

Inevitability: Since sexual orientation cannot be changed, gays inevitably will embrace it, because God intended it.

People identifying as gay Christians often recall their acceptance of homosexuality as a liberation, a turning point whereby they realized God refused their prayers for change because He never intended them to change. The inevitability argument, then, presumes that what's immune to change is divinely ordained and should be yielded to, even celebrated.

I've already addressed the false presumption of an agreed-upon definition of *sexual orientation,* as well as the unrealistic either/or definition of change, both of which this argument presumes.

Two other common misconceptions come into play here: If something is inborn, God must have created it, and if something is immutable, God must condone it. Both are unbiblical.

FIRST RESPONSE: **The argument defines sexual responses as either/or, without considering primary and secondary responses.**

As the American Psychological Association has acknowledged, sexual responses in people occur on a continuum, rather than as strictly either homo- or heterosexual. Many people have a *primary* attraction to one sex, with a *secondary* attraction to the other.

Before the actress Anne Heche, for example, began a lesbian relationship with Ellen DeGeneres, she'd never been attracted to women, but she felt a strong pull toward Ellen.[16] After their breakup, Miss Heche returned to relations with men, and she's now a married mother. Her primary attractions seem to be heterosexual, with capacity for a secondary homosexual response.

Numbers of Christian men and women who are attracted to the same sex have primary and secondary responses as well. Having turned from homosexual behavior in obedience to God, they realize a potential for response to the opposite sex under the right circumstances. Their secondary heterosexual response may not be as strong, or come as quickly, as their primary homosexual one. But having closed the door on homosexual relations, and having found someone they genuinely love and want to partner with, they become primarily attracted to their spouse *emotionally*, while still attracted to the same sex *erotically*. So they invest in their primary emotional and secondary erotic response and find greater satisfaction and peace doing so.

One site describes the experience like this:

Both sexual and romantic attraction can be broken down into two components: Primary and Secondary. . . .

Primary attraction is attraction based off of easily available information—looks, smell, etc. It requires very little time, and is more based on first impressions and/or physical features.

Secondary attraction is attraction that is based on the relationship/emotional connection with another person, and typically develops over longer periods of time. It is more based on the knowledge of a personality and/or shared experiences.[17]

In that sense they're not unlike many married people who are less attracted to their spouses than they might be to others, but are still wholly committed to their marriage and love their spouses deeply, never dreaming of breaking their bond. Their primary sexual attraction may be to other people they see and interact with. But they resist their primary responses and invest in their secondary ones, which is congruent with their faith and priorities. And in the process, the secondary response sometimes grows to become their primary one.

A marriage without sexual attraction seems wrong, since marriage is a sexual covenant, the erotic union being an important part of it. For that reason I strongly advise people who've repented of homosexual behavior *not* to marry unless and until they feel specific sexual (not just emotional) attractions to the person they're considering for a spouse. Some—many, in fact—find that the primary/secondary model applies. And if therapy or counsel assists in such a process, then it is effective treatment, awakening unrecognized potentials, and legitimate change does occur.

Second Response: **Traditionalists hold to a different framework defining change.**

When I repented of homosexuality in 1984, both as behavior and identification, I immediately changed.

Not in my feelings, but in my mindset. I had gone from disobedient to *obedient*, and that seismic shift—from *I will* to *Thy will*—remains one of the most enormous changes of my life.

This is where Traditionalists and Revisionists tend to talk past each other. To many Revisionists, sexual attraction alone determines sexual orientation. So a person who retains any attraction to the same sex remains homosexual, regardless of any changes in identity, behavior, or even strength of attractions.

Traditionalists, framing concepts of change in biblical terms, look at other elements to determine change: obedience versus disobedience, ongoing shedding of other sinful patterns, improved relational capacities, and clear conscience before God. Those are legitimate biblical markers for determining if someone is changing. Within this framework, we presume temptations toward a former sin will continue, though what each believer experiences varies. Still, we presume change has occurred if the individual no longer practices, identifies with, or lives under the power of a sin.

The Revisionist comfortable with his homosexuality says, "My orientation is homosexual."

The Traditionalist tempted by homosexuality is less inclined to speak in terms of orientation, saying instead, "My identity is Christian, my priority is Christ, and I strive to run the race well. In the process I may experience homosexual temptations, which neither define nor rule me, along with plenty of other temptations. And by the grace of God, I withstand them."

THIRD RESPONSE: God may allow ongoing struggles without intending that we be overcome by them.

Paul was beset by something so vexing he described it as a "messenger of Satan" and a "thorn in the flesh" (2 Cor. 12:7), which he begged God to remove, to no avail. God made it clear that Paul's ability to continue his life and ministry with this thorn would glorify Him, and that His grace would be sufficient to see Paul through his struggles (12:9).

He prayed for God to change him. God didn't. Yet he was expected to live his life fully, all the more reliant on God's grace because of the condition he was allowed to deal with.

Modern examples of "thorns" abound, and an ongoing struggle with sexual desires is no doubt one of them.

Immorality: Attempts to change sexual orientation are damaging and should be outlawed.

In February 2015 a New Jersey judge ruled that a therapist's claims that homosexuality is a curable disorder were fraudulent, based on the state's Consumer Fraud Act.[18] An online petition to President Obama requested that he make reparative therapy illegal.[19] And legislation known as the Therapeutic Fraud Prevention Act was introduced in May 2015 to ban the practice entirely in California.[20]

The trend will continue, and new waves of debates will consider, not just whether homosexuality can be changed, but also whether therapeutic attempts to change it are harmful and should be outlawed.

A kneejerk cry of "persecution" is understandable but should be avoided. Believers champion freedom of speech, conscience, and religion, and at first glance these laws seem egregious violations of all three. But some people have been genuinely harmed by wrong approaches to homosexuality and recovery, and we should take seriously some of the damage claims from former clients or patients of reparative therapists or "ex-gay" ministries, as well as concerns raised by the American Psychological and Psychiatric Associations regarding the practice. We should be just as concerned with accepting and acting upon *legitimate* criticism as we are with examining and debunking *illegitimate* criticism.

For example, former clients of some groups or therapists have claimed their treatment involved undressing,[21] sexual experimentations with women, ingestion of Viagra, or advice to cut off family relationships without cause.[22]

Since it's difficult to prove what did or did not happen in a therapist's office, much less what was or wasn't said, claims of former clients should be scrutinized. But if they are accurate, they constitute legitimate, serious complaints. For that reason, the Traditionalist position toward laws banning reparative therapy should be clear but informed. To this end, the rest of this chapter offers further clarification of balanced thinking about therapeutic methods for treating unwanted homosexuality.

Traditional Position 2

Professional assistance should be available for people in conflict over their sexuality and should be practiced using sound professional guidelines.

Revisionist Argument 1

All major mental health organizations agree that reparative therapy damages people.

Revisionists often, in my experience, express the negative general tone of the mental health professions toward reparative therapy as if it were an unqualified condemnation, which is not quite accurate.

FIRST RESPONSE: The American Psychiatric Association has said otherwise.

In their official statements on reparative therapy, the association says, "To date, there are no scientifically rigorous outcome studies to determine either the actual efficacy or harm of 'reparative treatments.'"[23] Clearly they do not support the practice, but just as clearly they admit having no scientifically verifiable proof that it's harmful.

Regarding complaints of harm, they also note, "The literature consists of anecdotal reports of individuals who have claimed to change, people who claim that attempts to change were harmful to them, and others who claimed to have changed and then later recanted those claims."[24]

Numbers of people claiming something was harmful to them is insufficient evidence, if their claims are the *only* evidence. This is especially true when the issue is as politically and socially charged as this one. With due respect and compassion to anyone truly harmed by former therapists and ministry leaders, we should note that upon examination it seems most plaintiffs reversed their position on homosexuality before declaring the therapy or help was damaging. The scenarios usually play something like this:

1. Individual goes to reparative therapist or ministry seeking help with unwanted homosexual attractions, believing homosexuality to be wrong and hoping for change.

2. After time, for any number of reasons, individual defaults to his homosexual desires.

3. Individual revises her beliefs to match and justify her behavior, embracing homosexuality as normal and right. Individual looks to gay-affirming resources for assurance he's made the right decision, finds encouragement for his choice and even to take action against his former therapist or ministry leader, receiving much support and even adulation from his newfound community.

4. Individual adopts oft-repeated line of thinking: "I was harmed by people telling me homosexuality's a sin, given false promises, told it was my fault I didn't change, and injured by the process."

Accepting the legitimacy of these complaints would be easier if the plaintiffs had not first made a major moral shift in their views on sexuality. Traditionalists who remained Traditonalists yet had complaints against prior therapists or ministries would be more credible.

But generally they don't, and as of this writing conclusive proof has not emerged showing that reparative therapy itself causes harm.

Second Response: **Abuses should be taken case by case.**

In cases of unprofessional conduct or a damaging approach, the courts should be involved on a case-by-case basis rather than by passing sweeping, unfair legislation. If it's proven that a reparative therapist damaged a client by unprofessional behavior, it hasn't logically been proven that reparative therapy itself is damaging.

Blanket condemnation of reparative therapy for the wrongs of a few practitioners makes no more sense than doing the same with any other type of therapy.

REVISIONIST ARGUMENT 2

Reparative therapy promises changes that don't occur.

The Revisionist website Faith in America voices a common complaint—that reparative therapists hurt people by "falsely promising gay people who are unhappy with their sexual orientation that they can become heterosexual. When gay men and women find that they can't change, they end up with feelings of guilt and failure that lead to depression, loss of friends and social support, addictive behaviors, and substance abuse."[25]

RESPONSE: **No, it doesn't, when presented and practiced responsibly.**

Dr. Nicolosi, unquestionably the leading proponent of reparative therapy, makes much more modest promises. On his website he states, "We are available to help men and women who want to decrease their same-sex attraction and to develop their opposite-sex potential."[26]

Claiming to "decrease same-sex attraction" and "develop opposite-sex potential" is a far cry from "promising gay people . . . they can become heterosexual." Freud himself, while skeptical about the possibility of fully converting a homosexual into a heterosexual, said he felt analysis could at times revive "the blighted germs of heterosexual tendencies, which are present in every homosexual."[27]

I myself was mistakenly described as a reparative therapist in a 1990 *Los Angeles Times* article, though the interview also quoted me as specifically saying I disliked the term. In the same interview, discussing outcomes of my work, I stated, "No one has ever left therapy saying, 'Wow, I have absolutely no homosexual thoughts or fantasies.'"[28]

If a therapist, ministry leader, or parachurch organization promises a complete change of sexual feelings, they are wrong. If they promise tools for managing sexual feelings and support for the goals of a Christian dealing with such feelings, they are right.

Toward a Reasonable Understanding of Change

Remember that not too many decades ago homosexuals were forced into psychiatric treatment, up to and including shock treatment and long-term, involuntary hospitalization. The specter of those days no doubt hangs over many when picturing reparative therapy, not realizing such therapy is only for the highly committed who share the worldview of the therapist. So the reaction from some is understandable.

But it's also difficult not to see much of the current rhetoric as more political than noble. A casual review of psychiatry's history shows countless abuses perpetrated by practitioners on unsuspecting patients for any number of other valid or invalid psychological issues. These exploiters have been disciplined, sued, or otherwise acted against, but no one's suggested the entire psychiatric industry be shut down because of these few. Abuses should be addressed case by case, correcting the individual who's wrong without punishing the collective.

As the cries for shutting down all reparative therapists increase, I hope that the American public responds with common sense and fairness.

Ten Talking Points about Change

1. *Sexual orientation* is not clearly defined, making realistic change hard to define as well.

2. *Reparative therapy* is a term often misapplied. It technically refers only to licensed therapists operating in a clinical setting from an analytic treatment model.

3. While major mental health organizations hold a prohomosexual view, they currently admit the absence of scientifically verifiable proof that reparative therapy causes harm.

4. Traditionalists believe homosexual behavior can be stopped and homosexual identity rejected. Homosexual temptations may persist, and responsible counseling and ministry recognize that.

5. Change of behavior is definite and significant change, as recognized when addicts or alcoholics stop using their drug.

6. When sexual temptations are consistently resisted, they often lose much power, diminishing in frequency or intensity. This, too, constitutes "change."

7. People may change by discovering potential for heterosexual attraction, even if it's secondary to homosexual attraction.

8. It is unfair and inaccurate to accuse all who help repentant homosexuals of promising complete reversal of homosexual attractions.

9. Complaints against a counselor or minister should be examined case by case. Reparative therapy should not be banned due to the unethical or unprofessional conduct of only a few.

10. Traditionalists who are same-sex attracted are entitled to professional assistance aligning with their worldview and goals. It should be forced upon no one, nor denied to anyone who wants it.

SAME-SEX MARRIAGE

> The attempt to redefine the family as a purely voluntary ar-
> rangement grows out of the modern delusion that people can
> keep all their options open all the time.
>
> —Christopher Lasch

This dispute's been with us longer than we think.

In 1970 the Reverend Troy Perry, founder of the pro-gay
Universal Fellowship of Metropolitan Community Churches,
filed a lawsuit against the State of California on behalf of lesbian
couple Neva Heckman and Judith Bellew, whose wedding he'd
officiated one year earlier.[1] The suit demanded state recognition
of their marriage and was dismissed almost immediately.

It was an opening shot, beginning a forty-five-year conflict
culminating in the US Supreme Court's decision that the Reverend Perry was right after all.

We've embarked on a massive social experiment, with the
2015 SCOTUS decision hailed by Revisionists as the new
Brown v. the Board of Education and mourned by Traditionalists

as the new *Roe v. Wade*. This can be compared to our decision decades ago to sanction no-fault divorce, believing (with little evidence) that it was the most humane action, beneficial to unhappy couples, and hopefully causing no harm to kids. Elucidating the long-term consequences of this well-intended risk, Dr. Judith Wallerstein of the University of California at Berkeley remarks, "We made radical changes in the family without realizing how it changes the experience of growing up. We embarked on a gigantic social experiment without any idea about how the next generation would be affected."[2]

And so it continues, another risk taken for the preferences of a few adults without adequate consideration of the long-term effects on children, marriage, and society. Yet gays can't be blamed for marriage's decline, since its erosion happened with no help from them long before they were included in its definition. The slide started when we decided its basic Judeo-Christian definition was negotiable.

Both Genesis and Jesus testify to the fourfold pillars that define marriage: a male-female union, independence, monogamy, and permanence. Referring to the Genesis account of the first union, Jesus said, "Have you not read that He who made them at the beginning 'made them male and female,' and said, 'For this reason a man shall leave his father and mother and be joined to his wife, and the two shall become one flesh'? So then, they are no longer two but one flesh. Therefore what God has joined together, let not man separate" (Matt. 19:4–6).

The 1970s saw us chipping away at these pillars by making marriages easier to exit and allowing porn and public infidelities to foster a casual acceptance of adultery. The recent redefinition of marriage is another downward step.

The New Selma

The experiment has graduated to the status of a movement. Same-sex marriage isn't just a new social development. To many, it's a fresh civil rights frontier.

As public opinion has shifted in favor of same-sex marriage, it has also developed a growing antipathy toward those opposing the shift. And that antipathy is erupting into a relentless, systematic backlash. In 2010 *National Review* observed the trend, warning, "The most influential of Americans, particularly those in law and the media, have been coming increasingly to regard opposition to same-sex marriage as irrational at best and bigoted at worst."[3]

When a culture's influencers decide opponents of same-sex marriage are no different from 1960s segregationists who opposed civil rights, the national feeling toward those opponents can't help but sour. Convince the public that a group is hateful, and the public's indignation toward that group will lead to legal and social overhauls. Abraham Lincoln described this unchanging principle: "In this and like communities, public sentiment is everything. With public sentiment, nothing can fail; without it nothing can succeed. Consequently he who moulds public sentiment, goes deeper than he who enacts statutes, or pronounces decisions."[4]

Yet this public sentiment is based not only on opinion but, according to some, on need as well—the need for a cause, the desire to champion the oppressed and right wrongs.

It's understandable. Seeing footage of the Allies liberating European concentration camps when I was in school, I felt revulsion at the crime, but a certain envy for the cause. I became fascinated with the WWII underground movements, full of young people risking everything to shelter persecuted Jews and resist the Nazi evil. And I longed for something to give my life such heroic meaning.

But chances for heroism aren't easily found, leaving a need unsatisfied. So young people today view footage of Dr. King's heroic Selma marches, standing up against systemic evil, with a similar envy, longing for a noble cause in which to enlist, a group to protect.

Hans Fiene calls this "Selma Envy," describing his fellow millennials as

> linking the civil-rights movement with the push for gay acceptance without pausing for a second to consider the comparison. We will continue diminishing the bravery of Rosa Parks by claiming a seat beside her as our reward for the one time we boycotted Chick-Fil-A for a month. We will trivialize the death of Medgar Evers by praising his blood for freeing gay couples to financially ruin a florist who hurt their feelings instead of walking one more block to find another purveyor of petunias who was happy to take their money.[5]

Compare Fiene's 2015 observations to the game plan of homosexual authors Marshall Kirk and Hunter Madsen sixteen years earlier for soliciting sympathy for gays: "Portray gays as victims of circumstance and depression, not as aggressive challengers.... Gays must be portrayed as victims in need of protection so that straights will be inclined by reflex to adopt the role of protector."[6]

Touchdown! The gay rights movement has convinced much of the public that homosexuals are victims deserving and needing protection, and the public's need for a heroic cause is satisfied. Against this backdrop, one of the most controversial things you can say is, "I still believe marriage is exclusively a male-female union."

Traditional Position

The only form of marriage condoned throughout Scripture is monogamous, permanent, and heterosexual. Marriage by this definition is best suited for raising children, meeting the deepest needs of both partners, and stabilizing society.

REVISIONIST ARGUMENT 1

Same-sex marriage causes no damage to children.

"The evidence to date suggests that home environments provided by lesbian and gay parents are as likely as those provided by heterosexual parents to support and enable children's psychosocial growth," the American Psychological Association maintains.[7] The American Psychiatric Association concurs: "The APA has recognized the importance of stable, same-sex relationships for the mental health of gay and lesbian people, families and the community through its 2000 Position Statement on Same-sex Civil Unions and its 2002 Position Statement on Adoption and Co-Parenting of Children by Same-sex Couples."[8] The American Academy of Pediatrics, the National Association of Social Workers, and the American Psychoanalytic Association take the same position.[9] With expert assurances from throughout the mental health industry, it's easy to assume the results of same-sex and opposite-sex parenting are virtually the same.

FIRST RESPONSE: **Not all experts agree on the effects of same-sex parenting.**

In 2012 Mark Regnerus, associate professor of sociology at the University of Texas at Austin, released his comprehensive

New Family Structures Study, which studied young adults aged eighteen to thirty-nine, raised in "different types of family arrangements with varying household experiences."[10] His conclusions were significant and controversial: When compared with offspring from married, intact mother-father homes, children raised in same-sex homes were more likely to

- experience poor educational attainment
- report overall lower levels of happiness and mental and physical health
- have impulsive behavior
- be in counseling or mental health therapy
- suffer from depression
- have recently thought of suicide
- identify as bisexual, lesbian, or gay
- have a sexually transmitted infection
- drink with intention of getting drunk
- smoke tobacco and marijuana
- plead guilty to minor legal offenses

Reaction to his study was swift and furious, but according to Peter Wood, president of the National Association of Scholars, "The effort to marginalize Regnerus's *SSR* article was not originally prompted by doubts about his methods, but by visceral dislike of his study findings."[11]

Regnerus wasn't the only researcher questioning the results of same-sex parenting. Australian sociologist Sotirios Sarantalos studied 174 primary school children raised by married heterosexual couples, same-sex couples, and cohabiting couples, and reported that "married [heterosexual] couples seem to offer the best environment for a child's social and educational development."[12]

David Cramer reviewed twenty studies showing more positive outcomes of same-sex parenting and found them lacking control groups and using sample groups that were either too small or too uniform.[13] Other concerns by researchers analyzing such studies included "lack of external validity," "major deficiencies in sampling," and personal investment of the subjects (same-sex parents) in a positive outcome from the study.[14]

We'd prefer, of course, to accept the word of professional bodies like the American Psychiatric Association and the American Psychological Association. But while recognizing their expertise, we also recognize the substantial influence their own gay advocacy groups have within the organizations. (The American Psychological Association has its Lesbian, Gay, Bisexual and Transgender Concerns office; the American Psychiatric Association has its Gay, Lesbian and Bisexual Caucus; the American Academy of Pediatrics has its LGBT Health and Wellness Division.) Remembering the effect gay lobbying had on the American Psychiatric Association's landmark decision to declassify and thereby normalize homosexuality in 1973, we're reminded of Dr. Ronald Bayer's comments on the process leading to that decision:

> The entire process, from the first confrontation organized by gay demonstrators . . . seemed to violate the most basic expectations about how questions of science should be resolved. Instead of being engaged in sober discussion of data, psychiatrists were swept up in a political controversy. The result was not a conclusion based on an approximation of the scientific truth as dictated by reason, but was instead an action demanded by the ideological temper of the times.[15]

If intense lobbying from gay advocacy groups could produce something as profound as a change in the American Psychiatric Association's diagnostic manual, we have to view their other (and lesser) statements and decisions regarding homosexuality with a certain skepticism.

All of which seriously calls into question our confidence that the effects of same-sex parenting are essentially the same as opposite-sex parenting.

Second Response: Research shows biological parenting is in the child's best interest.

No one's saying that same-sex couples always do overt damage to children. Homosexual parents can offer love, structure, and valuable guidance to kids, and in many cases provide a healthier home than some heterosexuals do. But comparing a best-case gay scenario to a worst-case straight one doesn't answer the bottom-line question: Can a relatively healthy gay or lesbian couple give children all that a relatively healthy heterosexual couple can?

We say no, not because of the parents' homosexuality, but because of their sameness. Two men or two women simply can't bring to the table what a man and a woman can. And studies conducted by researchers with a variety of ideological slants confirm this: fathers count, mothers count, and biology counts.

Fathers Count

When analyzing over one hundred studies examining the impact of biological fathers on children, Ronald Rohner and Robert Veneziano concluded, "Overall, father love appears to be as heavily implicated as mother love in offsprings' psychological well-being and health."[16]

And active father figures play a key role in reducing behavior problems in boys and psychological problems in young women, according to a 2008 review:

> Swedish researchers also found that regular positive contact reduces criminal behaviour among children in low-income families and enhances cognitive skills like intelligence, reasoning and language development. Children who lived with both a mother and father figure also had less behavioural problems than those who just lived with their mother. The review looked at 24 papers published between 1987 and 2007, covering 22,300 individual sets of data from 16 studies. 18 of the 24 papers also covered the social economic status of the families studied.[17]

Dr. Anna Sarkadi, the review's primary author, said,

> We found various studies that showed that children who had positively involved father figures were less likely to smoke and get into trouble with the police, achieved better levels of education and developed good friendships with children of both sexes. Long-term benefits included women who had better relationships with partners and a greater sense of mental and physical well-being.[18]

Mothers Count

A study released in the *Journal of Family Issues* concluded that maternal employment during a child's adolescent years significantly decreases grades, underscoring the specialized nature of maternal care.[19]

In summary, David Popenoe affirms the importance of both parents: "We should disavow the notion that 'mommies can make good daddies,' just as we should disavow the popular notion of radical feminists that 'daddies can make good mommies.'

. . . The two sexes are different to the core, and each is necessary—culturally and biologically—for the optimal development of a human being."[20]

Biology Counts

When comparing the ties between stepparents and stepchildren to those between biological parents and their offspring, the results are clear and unsurprising: where childrearing is concerned, biology counts. Some examples:

- "An extensive body of research tells us that children do best when they grow up with both biological parents in a low-conflict marriage. . . . Thus, it is not simply the presence of two parents, as some have assumed, but the presence of two biological parents that seems to support child development."[21]
- "It has been consistently found that stepfamilies are not as close as nuclear families (Kennedy, 1985; Pill, 1990) and that stepparent-stepchild relationships are not as emotionally close as parent-child relationships."[22]
- "Most researchers now agree that together these studies support the notion that, on average, children do better when raised by two married, biological parents who have low-conflict relationships."[23]

If research indicates that being raised by one's biological father and mother provides the optimal environment, why would we then suggest that a structure that by its very nature cannot do so could prove just as effective?

Self-identified liberal Democrat David Blankenhorn, president of the New York–based Institute for American Values, seems to wonder the same:

Marriage is a gift that society bestows on the next generation. Marriage (and only marriage) unites the three core dimensions of parenthood—biological, social, and legal—into one pro-child form: the married couple. Marriage says to a child: The man and the woman whose sexual union made you will also be there to love and raise you. Marriage says to society as a whole: For every child born, there is a recognized mother and father, accountable to the child and to each other.[24]

His conclusion seems the only truly logical one: "All our scholarly instruments seem to agree: For healthy development, what a child needs more than anything else is the mother and father who together made the child, who love the child and love each other."[25]

REVISIONIST ARGUMENT 2

Same-sex marriage does no harm to heterosexual couples.

Maybe the commonest response to the Traditionalist view is, "What's it to you?"

Celebrities have been especially adept at posing this question. Clint Eastwood, for example, asks, "These people who are making a big deal out of gay marriage? I don't give a —— about who wants to get married to anybody else! Just give everybody the chance to have the life they want." Rapper Jay-Z adds, "What people do in their own homes is their business, and you can choose to love whoever you love." And singer Janet Jackson summarizes, "It's two people that are in love with one another. What's the issue?"[26]

The marriage of two same-sex people, according to this argument, has no effect at all on heterosexual couples. At first glance this seems logical; if someone else marries, how does that hurt me? But we should consider some effects of marriage's redefinition.

RESPONSE: The redefinition of marriage leads also to redefinitions of faithfulness and commitment that do affect heterosexual couples.

Homosexual couples certainly don't attack or inflict immediate harm on heterosexual ones, and no one's suggesting they do. But if certain principles and practices are common to same-sex couples, and same-sex couples come under the "marriage" tent with heterosexuals, couldn't their principles and practices influence heterosexual couples and their families?

Some homosexuals openly declare they would, and should. More than two decades ago, respected gay journalist Andrew Sullivan described the "beneficial" influence the nonmonogamous ethic of many gay couples would have on straight couples. Referring to the practice of allowing sex outside their partnerships, he stated, "There is more likely to be greater understanding of the need for extramarital outlets between two men than between a man and a woman. . . . But something of the gay's relationship's necessary honesty, its flexibility, and its equality could undoubtedly help strengthen and inform many heterosexual bonds."[27]

Translation: Heterosexual husbands, take a cue from nonmonogamous gay men. Open marriage can be fun.

The influence of gay couples upon straight ones may not be intentional. And then again, it might. The provocative activist Michelangelo Signorile admitted, "A middle ground might be to fight for same-sex marriage and its benefits and then, once granted, redefine the institution of marriage completely, to demand the right to marry not as a way of adhering to society's moral codes but rather to debunk a myth and radically alter an archaic institution."[28]

And a year before that, lesbian Paula Ettelbrick claimed,

> Arguing for the right to legal marriage, lesbians and gay men would be forced to claim that we are just like heterosexual couples, have the same goals and purposes, and vow to structure our lives similarly. . . . We must keep our eyes on the goals of providing true alternatives to marriage and of radically reordering society's view of reality.[29]

Tellingly, *New York* magazine reported in 2005, "Many straight couples struggling with [monogamy] issues look to gay male friends, for whom a more fluid notion of commitment is practically the norm."[30] The article describes a heterosexual husband's desire to make his marriage "open" after hearing his gay friend describe his own sexual pursuits outside his committed relationship.[31]

And such pursuits do seem to be business as usual among many gay men. A 2010 study at San Francisco State University observed 556 male couples for three years, finding that 50 percent of them had agreements that sex outside their relationship was acceptable.[32]

Admitting that "none of this is news in the gay community, but few will speak publicly about it," the article includes comments from gay therapist and author Joe Quirk, who sees nonmonogamy as not only healthy for gay men but an example straight couples could follow: "That [nonmonogamous] transparency can make relationships stronger. The combination of freedom and mutual understanding can foster a unique level of trust. The traditional American marriage is in crisis, and we need insight. If innovation in marriage is going to occur, it will be spearheaded by homosexual marriages."[33]

Please reread that last sentence: *"If innovation in marriage is going to occur, it will be spearheaded by homosexual marriages."*

Which makes columnist Steven Thrasher's question all the more relevant: "Will straight America learn from 'gay marriage' and become more open, more sexually conversant, more queer?"[34]

Some Revisionists hope so. Hanna Rosin, writing about the "dirty little secret" that most gay couples aren't monogamous, said wistfully, "In some far-off, ideal world, this kind of openness may infect the straight world, and heterosexual couples may actually start to tackle the age-old problem of boring monogamous sex. But do any of us really believe that?"[35]

Sadly, yes. Some of us are beginning to.

REVISIONIST ARGUMENT 3

Same-sex marriage poses no risk to personal freedoms.

We commonly hear, "If you disagree, that's OK, nobody's going to force you."

So Whoopi Goldberg quipped, "You know, I understand not everybody is for gay marriage. But if you're not for gay marriage, don't marry a gay person. That's what I say."[36] And President Obama took a conciliatory tone toward Traditionalists while celebrating the SCOTUS same-sex marriage decision: "We know that Americans of good will continue to hold a wide range of views on this issue. Opposition in some cases is based on sincere and deeply held beliefs. All of us who welcome today's news should be mindful of that fact, recognize different viewpoints, revere our commitment to religious freedom."[37]

"We want same-sex marriage," gays seem to say. "You disagree? Fine, leave us alone, and we'll leave you alone. We'll coexist because we're a tolerant movement within a pluralistic culture."

But in the interest of honesty, someone should add, "Unless, of course, you don't cooperate."

RESPONSE: **The damage has already begun.**

Space here prohibits the listing of bakeries, restaurants, florists, caterers, facility owners, and photographers who've been forced to shut down, sued, fined, or subjected to vicious social attacks because they declined to service a same-sex wedding. Just google the subject, and the facts will pop up.

It's established that private secular businesses have to cater events to which they may in conscience object. Religious institutions are almost certainly next, considering President Obama's attorney's admission. When asked by Supreme Court Justice Samuel Alito whether Christian colleges supporting traditional marriage would be forced to offer housing to homosexual couples if marriage was redefined, Solicitor General Donald Verrilli replied, "It's certainly going to be an issue. I don't deny that."[38]

Time will show that to be an enormous understatement. When gay legislation challenges religious freedom, images of the schoolyard bully and the skinny kid come to mind. We've consistently seen, this past decade, a push, not for true diversity, but for monolithic approval of homosexuality, with any dissent being silenced by coercion or marginalized to voicelessness.

So only the most naïve or poorly informed would assume the legitimizing of same-sex marriage won't be accompanied by increased sanctions against anyone objecting to it. Our embrace of same-sex marriage does and will restrict the freedoms of individuals, businesses, organizations, and churches. And while the average citizen who condones it won't be affected (what bully picks on his supporters?), the test of whether a trend is benign is hardly the way it treats it supporters. Its integrity is shown by its response to its detractors.

Gregory Cochran of California Baptist University gets to the bottom line of all this nicely:

> Here is tyranny. If the government can go against biological nature and prescribe rights to groups of citizens without recourse to a reality outside of itself, then government has become god. Government not only will give rights to some, it will take rights from others. Not only will the government make laws consistent with its revised reality; it will also—of necessity—enforce those laws for the sake of maintaining its ability to control reality. Reality itself will become what the government mandates.[39]

Ten Talking Points about Same-Sex Marriage

1. Same-sex couples cannot give children what opposite-sex couples can. Each sex carries innate parenting skills that, when combined, produce a benefit that two men or two women cannot provide.

2. Children do better when raised by a male and female. They do best when raised by their biological father and mother.

3. Studies indicate children raised by same-sex couples are more susceptible to certain emotional and behavioral difficulties.

4. A high percentage of gay male couples are nonmonogamous by mutual agreement. Defining their relationships

as marriage devalues the fourfold definition of the covenant as independent, monogamous, permanent, and heterosexual.

5. The practice of nonmonogamy among gay male couples may influence heterosexual husbands to consider similar practices in their own marriages, introducing instability into more marriages and, by extension, into society. The stability of a culture's marriages affects its stability in general.

6. Some prohomosexual apologists have openly declared their intention to use the redefinition of marriage as a tool for overhauling our concepts of marriage in general.

7. The validity of many mental health associations' approval of same-sex marriage is mitigated by the facts that they have pro-gay divisions within, openly support prohomosexual political and social causes, and have proven susceptible to lobbying, even sacrificing standard research and deliberation practices.

8. The redefinition of marriage has already introduced a wave of legal actions against private businesses and organizations declining to support it by their participation.

9. It will be virtually impossible, having removed the male-female prerequisite for marriage, to avoid eventually introducing polygamy into the definition as well.

10. What God established from the beginning can be redefined but never redesigned. Attempts to mimic created intent must by their nature fall short of success.

HOMOPHOBIA, HATE, HYPOCRISY, AND HARM

"When I use a word," Humpty Dumpty said in rather a scornful tone, "it means just what I choose it to mean—neither more nor less."

—Lewis Carroll, *Alice in Wonderland*

To portray someone as hateful or harmful, you should have to prove their hatefulness.

But if it can't be proven, the next best tactic is to arbitrarily decide how *hate* and *harm* are defined, then apply that definition to them. Because whoever controls the definition of terms wins the debate.

That subjects the "hateful" parties to being misquoted or misrepresented, as Jesus was when He predicted the destruction of "this temple," meaning His body (John 2:19–21), then was later maligned as planning to destroy the Jerusalem temple (Mark 14:57–58). Or as Paul was when he accompanied Gentile believers to Jerusalem and was wrongfully accused of promoting the overthrow of Jewish law and improperly bringing Gentiles into the temple (Acts 21:26–29).

Peter warned believers that some would think it "strange" that Christians didn't "run with them in the same flood of dissipation" and would thereby be "speaking evil" of them (1 Pet. 4:4). And one of the most effective ways to speak evil of someone is to define what they do as hateful or destructive.

This is done to Traditionalists by painting them as homophobic, hateful, hypocritical, or harmful, and as we've seen, a large percentage of the public is convinced that this portrait is accurate. So in this chapter we'll examine some of the commonest ways those accusations are made and how best to respond.

Traditional Position

Calling homosexuality a sin is a statement of belief, and there is no implicit or explicit hatred, much less phobia or harm, in that belief.

REVISIONIST ARGUMENT 1

Homophobia: The Traditionalist position is phobic.

In 1972 psychologist George Weinberg coined the term *homophobia* to mean "dread of being in close quarters with homosexuals."[1] The term later broadened in use, eventually coming to refer to virtually any antihomosexual sentiment. Lately its use has diminished, so remarks critical of homosexuality are now commonly called "antigay," although the term *homophobia* is still widespread.

The word draws power from the growing belief that homophobia is a dreadful thing, but even more because it shifts possession of the pathology. The person who views homosexuality as abnormal finds *himself* labeled "homophobic"; the focus and diagnosis shifts from same-sex behavior to *objections* to same-sex behavior. These days, to be gay is largely seen as a simple preference. But to be homophobic is to be diseased.

FIRST RESPONSE: **Homophobia inaccurately applies a phobia.**

The term suggests that any objection to homosexuality is based on a psychological problem, rather than a reasonable worldview.

But there's nothing reasonable in presuming beliefs and phobias are the same. In fact, when a homosexual person slaps the label on me, I point out that I am standing close to him, engaging him, displaying none of the symptoms associated with phobias.

According to the Mayo Clinic, genuine phobic responses include the following:

- A feeling of uncontrollable panic, terror or dread when you're exposed to the source of your fear
- The feeling that you must do everything possible to avoid what you fear
- The inability to function normally because of your anxiety
- Physical as well as psychological reactions, including sweating, rapid heartbeat, difficulty breathing, a feeling of panic and intense anxiety[2]

If I'm exhibiting none of these symptoms while talking face-to-face in close proximity to a homosexual person, then I clearly don't have the condition known as homophobia. Few people do.

SECOND RESPONSE: **A phobic response to homosexuals is possible but rare.**

In fairness, a literally phobic response to homosexuals can and at times does occur. There are people deeply threatened by homosexuals, whether through their own revulsion or, perhaps, insecurity. And literal homophobia was probably more common, though less defined, in earlier years when homosexuality was considered an exotic abnormality.

But to slap the term onto Traditionalists in general is inaccurate. Gay commentator Andrew Sullivan, to his credit, acknowledges this:

> Perhaps the most depressing and fruitless feature of the current debate about homosexuality is to treat all versions of this argument as the equivalent of bigotry. They are not. In an appeal to "nature," the most persuasive form of this argument is rooted in one of the oldest traditions of thought in the West, a tradition that still carries a great deal of intuitive sense. . . . And at its most serious, it is not a phobia; it is an argument.[3]

REVISIONIST ARGUMENT 2

Hatred: Traditionalists are haters.

Hate is a powerful disqualifier. When you believe someone's words or positions are motivated by hatred, that nullifies their arguments, no matter how logical they might otherwise be.

So if Party A hates Party B, then any objections Party A has to Party B's behavior are easy to write off as hateful rantings. Whether or not A's objections are valid, Party A hates Party B, case closed.

Imagine, for example, a member of ISIS criticizing Israel's national policies. The criticism could have merit, yet ISIS's unbridled hatred for Israel makes it virtually impossible to think anything they say about Jews isn't motivated, and tainted, by malice.

This dynamic works on a number of levels. First, the person wrestling with her own sexuality finds it easier to ignore Christian objections to homosexuality if, in her mind, those objections are hate-based. That's a hurdle most Traditionalists have to jump when speaking to a homosexual person, because many of them approach the conversation already convinced that we hate them.

It works on the broader scale as well. The gay rights movement has benefitted immeasurably by convincing the public that moral objections to homosexuality aren't moral at all but hate-based, thereby discrediting the goals, beliefs, and members of any group that so objects. Neutralizing them will be easy after that.

Consider the way you'd feel if the Ku Klux Klan set up shop in your neighborhood. Believing in freedom of speech, you grudgingly might acknowledge their right to be there. But you'd almost certainly loathe their presence, and probably them as well.

Now suppose some outraged citizen set fire to their shop and destroyed it. Would you sympathize with the shop owner?

Doubtful. You might technically believe it was wrong to destroy their business. But the inherent evil of their message would probably leave you indifferent to the fact they were stripped of their right to purvey it.

So don't underestimate the power of the "hater" label. It's being used to convince the public that you, if you're a Traditionalist, belong in the same category as the KKK.

That's a clever and manipulative form of maligning, but honest misunderstanding plays into this as well. Many lesbians and gays sincerely believe Traditionalists hate them. No cynicism involved, just simple misunderstanding.

It's there for many reasons: The cruel remark a lesbian heard from a conservative Christian, whom she assumes—wrongly but somewhat logically—represents all Christians. Or the terrible bullying a gay man suffered at the hands of schoolmates or peers who attended church but were wildly un-Christian in fact. Or the endlessly looping message in the media, over the internet, or on campuses, repeating over and over, "Conservative Christians are haters, conservative Christians are haters."

All of this can leave a person convinced she or he is hated, making dialogue with that person a challenge.

I encountered that challenge as a guest speaker at Princeton Seminary in the 1990s. Asked to address homosexuality from a conservative position (with advance warning that the vast majority of professors and students attending would probably find my views odious), I arrived an hour beforehand.

What greeted me in the foyer was both amusing and disturbing. Tables had been set up as "places of safety" for students— gays and lesbians, in particular—who felt traumatized by my presentation, where they could process and debrief with a sympathetic volunteer if they felt damaged by the talk I was about to inflict on them.

Ironically, the talk I'd prepared was more a critique of conservative Christians than of homosexuality. In fact, my main points centered on the Traditionalists' need to repent of hostility toward homosexuals. No matter. The listeners' advance perception of me was of a hater, a mean-spirited fundamentalist spewing archaic, destructive ideas.

If that challenge was evident in the 1990s, it's surely more prevalent today.

RESPONSE: **Perception of hatred is not proof of hatred.**

In dialogue, I find it helpful to reference the definition of hatred per Webster's: "a very strong feeling of dislike" or "prejudiced hostility or animosity."[4]

Without an agreed-upon definition of hatred, we get nowhere. So long as the right to subjectively define a word remains at the discretion of Party A, then he, like Carroll's character quoted earlier, gets to decide whatever he wants a word to mean, leaving Party B unable to defend himself and rendering the conversation meaningless.

Yet simply asking if your friend thinks anything is morally wrong also helps clarify things. She's certain to answer yes, to which you can respond, "Do you hate everyone who does anything you consider morally wrong?"

By saying no, she'll prove your point.

It's possible, even common, to disapprove without hating. Most reasonable people agree that hate is an objective concept, easily defined, and that everyone believes some things are right and some wrong, and that belief and hate are not the same.

They'll further acknowledge that, while they believe some people do things that are wrong, that doesn't mean they hate those people. With that understanding, it's easy to show that moral objections to homosexuality don't qualify as hatred. The "hater" perception can be challenged—in most cases, effectively.

REVISIONIST ARGUMENT 3

*Hateful legacies: We've been wrong about
slavery, women, and racism.*

In explaining his change from a Traditional to Revisionist view, Brian McLaren, like countless others, compares historical

Christian support for slavery and segregation to modern support for the Traditional position. He does this by claiming he "eventually came to believe that just as the Western church had been wrong on slavery, wrong on colonialism, wrong on environmental plunder, wrong on subordinating women, wrong on segregation and apartheid (all of which it justified biblically) . . . we had been wrong on this issue."[5]

David Gushee pushes further, not only employing the same comparison, but asserting that within one hundred years "99% of all reasonable Christian human beings" will someday affirm the Revisionist view, just as we now affirm "the proper positions on slavery and Nazism and civil rights and Apartheid."[6]

It's an emotionally powerful argument, claiming that the church supported oppressive positions in the past, so history repeats itself when the church supports antihomosexual positions.

FIRST RESPONSE: **Not all Christians supported slavery or segregation, and both the abolitionist and civil rights movements were largely advanced by Christian thought.**

Christian leadership in the abolitionist movement is well documented, beginning with the Quakers' ban on slaveholding and the American Anti-Slavery Society, which largely drove early efforts to abolish the practice.[7] Without question many churches, including numerous Southern white churches, viewed the movement as evil. But without the efforts of Bible-believing abolitionists, the broader movement would have lost much of its strength. So to claim the Western church as a whole supported slavery, as McLaren does, is unreasonable and inaccurate. Much of it did; some of it didn't.

Likewise, to remove Dr. Martin Luther King Jr. from the American civil rights movement is akin to removing Paul the apostle from the book of Acts. But that removal is necessary if you claim the Christian population in the 1950s and 1960s was uniformly in favor of segregation. White Christians joined African Americans in desegregation efforts, efforts not limited to any one class or race.

As with slavery, many Christians supported twentieth-century racism via distortions of Scripture. The late Reverend Jerry Falwell admitted and regretted his defense of segregation,[8] as did the late influential Southern Baptist leader W. A. Criswell, who lamented, "Never had I been so blind."[9] Christian efforts to preserve slavery and segregation are a stain on church history we can't erase. But not all Christians of that era are tarnished with it.

SECOND RESPONSE: **Past errors don't disprove current positions.**

Many Christians were solidly on the wrong side of history regarding race.

The question is: Does that prove we're wrong about homosexuality? If you've been wrong in the past, is that proof you're wrong in the present?

Everyone has, at some time, been firmly convinced of something only to later find they had it all wrong. But that just proves *anyone* can be wrong. Human fallibility demands that we all think positions through carefully, even prayerfully. That's the wisdom and humility we can glean from past mistakes.

None of which prevents us, after careful examination, from achieving certainty about a view. Each issue has to be considered on its own merit, case by case. So yes, if I was wrong in the past, I could also be wrong in the present. Possibly, but not necessarily.

And it works both ways, or it doesn't work at all. If Traditionalists must abandon confidence in our positions because our track record is imperfect, then Revisionists must do the same. Which they won't and, in fact, they shouldn't. I grant them their right to be certain, whether or not they grant me the same.

All of us reserve the right to take positions based on careful analysis and conscience, regardless of past errors, whether errors of our own or of our forebears.

THIRD RESPONSE: **The Bible itself promotes neither slavery nor racism.**

Activist Dan Savage accused the Bible, not just Christians, of promoting slavery. He then asked how we can trust the Bible on something as complex as homosexuality when it got something as basic as racism wrong.[10]

But a careful reading of the Book cannot support his conclusions. Theologian Robert Gagnon points out that, while the Bible does not specifically prohibit slavery, "Scripture nowhere expresses a vested interest in preserving slavery, whereas Scripture does express a clear countercultural and creational vested interest in preserving an exclusive male-female dynamic to human sexual relationships."[11]

There are biblical guidelines for the treatment of slaves, mostly commanding fair treatment, but no mandate for slavery itself. Slavery, whether bodily bondage or spiritual bondage to sin or legalism, is something referred to negatively throughout the Bible (see, for example, Exod. 13:3; Deut. 26:6; Ezra 9:8; Neh. 5:5; Rom. 8:15; Gal. 4:9). And as for racism, you'd be hard-pressed to find a more succinct antiracist statement than Paul's affirmation that "there is neither Jew nor Greek, there is neither slave nor free, there is neither male nor female; for you are all one in Christ Jesus" (Gal. 3:28).

Also, though slavery itself (which was sometimes voluntary and often not racially based) is not condemned in Scripture, kidnapping people and forcing them into servitude is. Under Moses's law such an act warranted the death penalty (Exod. 21:16), and Paul reiterated this condemnation in 1 Timothy 1:8–10.

The Bible promotes neither slavery nor homosexuality. Christians have in times past promoted what Scripture doesn't, which Traditionalists should keep in mind without being inhibited from standing firm where Scripture stands firm. Sins of the past shouldn't weaken stands in the present.

REVISIONIST ARGUMENT 4

Hypocrisy: Traditionalists wink at divorce and remarriage but condemn homosexuality.

It's often pointed out that Traditionalists take Bible verses against homosexuality literally, while fudging on Jesus's condemnation of unbiblical divorce and remarriage (Matt. 5:32).

Sometimes Revisionists incorrectly state that all Christian remarriages violate Christ's teaching, ignoring the exception He made for adultery, calling our tolerance for any remarriage hypocrisy. Others point out how easily Christians divorce and remarry, even apart from adultery.

FIRST RESPONSE: **Remarriage can be valid.**

Matthew 5:32 prohibits remarriage if adultery didn't cause the divorce but says nothing about remarriage for those whose first union was terminated by unfaithfulness. "Serial" divorce and remarriage certainly shows a casual attitude toward marriage and warrants pastoral intervention, but remarriage can be valid. The Bible offers no such validity for homosexual union.

SECOND RESPONSE: **Two wrongs are still two wrongs.**

The wrongness of a heterosexual divorce or remarriage can't legitimize a homosexual relationship. If some churches are lax regarding divorce and remarriage, the solution is restoring faithfulness to Scripture regarding marriage, not ignoring Scripture regarding sexuality.

REVISIONIST ARGUMENT 5

Harm: Traditionalist teaching inflicts emotional damage.

Several gay advocates claim Traditionalist teaching emotionally injures homosexual people. Mel White said he prefers physical violence to the emotional violence of calling his relationship a sin.[12] David Gushee refers to Traditionalism as a "destructive paradigm."[13] And Judge Paul Walker, ruling on California's anti-same-sex marriage Proposition 8, went so far as to write in his ruling that "religious beliefs that gay and lesbian relationships are sinful or inferior to heterosexual relationships harm gays and lesbians."[14]

FIRST RESPONSE: **Offense isn't injury; disagreement isn't damage.**

The discomfort of being offended by an opposing viewpoint shouldn't be classified as "harmful." It's uncomfortable, certainly, just as Traditionalists vilified as "delusional" or "reactionary" feel uncomfortable. The high price of pluralism is the discomfort of hearing your view challenged or your way of life criticized. But no one is damaged solely because someone else assesses their behavior as sinful, just as no one is damaged solely by hearing their religious beliefs assessed as superstitious or downright stupid.

SECOND RESPONSE: **The method, not the message, may be harmful.**

Name-calling and denigration are harmful, so a lesbian or gay subjected to either has been harmed. Likewise, a Traditionalist ostracizing or humiliating a homosexual is wrong in his method of expression, but not necessarily in the view he expresses. Some of these wrong methods are legally protected by the First Amendment but still constitute sins in their own right, calling for repentance and maybe restitution. Others, such as libel, slander, and some forms of threats, constitute violations of legitimate law and deserve punishment by government authority. But none of these necessarily negates the moral position of the perpetrator. His methods, not his message, are where the wrong lies.

REVISIONIST ARGUMENT 6

Harm: Traditionalist teaching incites physical violence.

Mel White also indicted Traditional teaching for inciting the murder of a gay couple by two white supremacists.[15] When gay Matthew Shepherd was brutally killed in the notorious Wyoming case, newswoman Katie Couric insinuated that influential Christian organizations contributed to a climate encouraging the murder of gays.[16] And a number of celebrities, including comedienne Kathy Griffin, actress Wanda Sykes, and singer Lance Bass, blamed Christian views about homosexuality for an unfathomable 2010 series of gay teen suicides.[17]

But this argument presumes that Traditional positions encourage already unbalanced people to assault and even murder homosexuals.

FIRST RESPONSE: **Hatred needs no help.**

Some people hate homosexuals out of their own prejudices or insecurities. Biblical teaching has nothing to do with this; indeed, biblical teaching, including admonitions to love one's neighbor and live peacefully with all, forbids violence against gays. Haters may use a moral position as an excuse for violence or vile methods of expression, but the villain is the hatred, not the position.

Similarly, child abusers sometimes justify their abuse by citing biblical commands for parents to assume authority in the home. And spousal abusers may claim the biblical headship position, when in truth they're motivated by violent urges, not God's Word.

Raising children "in the training and admonition of the Lord" (Eph. 6:4) is not a command to abuse; "the husband is head of the wife" (5:23) is not an inducement to battering; and nothing in these verses excuses violence. Blame rests with a perversion of the teaching, not the teaching itself.

SECOND RESPONSE: **If moral instruction incites violence, why isn't there widespread violence?**

If teaching that something is morally wrong encourages violence against the wrongdoers, it logically follows that Christians would routinely be assaulting gossips, fornicators, gluttons, and indeed everyone guilty of any biblical sin. Since that obviously isn't happening, it's equally obvious that teaching something is sin does not incite assault on the sinner.

When you, without malice, hold beliefs that are also without malice, it's hard having malicious motives dishonestly assigned to you by someone who's inconvenienced by your stance. The injustice is even harder to swallow when that person is sincere in believing you're truly hateful and potentially harmful just because you won't abandon doctrines that seem so obviously true and clear.

Traditionalists, though, can expect this to continue as our position is increasingly distorted and despised by some, or perhaps by most. We can expect to deal increasingly with minority status accompanied by unbridled contempt and unreasonable hostility, often coming from seemingly reasonable people who should know better. It's time to accept that as part of today's social and doctrinal tensions.

But you can also find people with whom you can reason, and you can always find opportunities to offer a loving, intelligent articulation of truth, and thereby counter the negative stereotypes others hold toward you. Some will wholly reject your views but also come to realize you're not hateful or harmful; in the process they will gain a more accurate view of biblical morality. Others will respond more redemptively, experiencing a change in their own beliefs through a quickening of conscience or a softening of heart.

Some will call you a hater. Some will love you for your willingness to be hated. And some will literally and eternally be turned, because you decided that faithfulness in sowing the seed was more important than worrying about the occasional tare.

All because you dared take Paul up on his challenge to be "able to teach" (2 Tim. 2:24).

Ten Talking Points about Homophobia, Hate, Hypocrisy, and Harm

1. The term *homophobia* misinterprets a moral position as a phobic response, even in the absence of phobic symptoms.

2. *Hate* is technically defined as a very strong feeling of dislike, or prejudiced hostility or animosity. The burden should rest on the accuser to prove hatred, not on the accused to prove innocence.

3. A perception of hatred is not proof of hatred.

4. Some Christians were wrong about slavery and racism, but this does not justify inaccurate and irresponsible claims that all Christians were guilty of the same sins.

5. Christians played a vital role in overturning slavery and in the civil rights movement. These righteous representatives of Christ weaken the accusation of all Christians being guilty of racism.

6. The Bible does not promote slavery but recognizes it and offers guidelines for fairer treatment of slaves, while speaking negatively about both slavery and bondage.

7. The fact that some Christians were wrong in the past hardly proves that Christians are wrong in the present. Past mistakes don't prove that current positions are wrong, because everyone has been wrong at some time.

8. If some Christians have hypocritically condemned homosexuality but winked at casual divorce, the answer is not to continue lowering the standards but, rather, to pay closer attention to *all* of them.

9. When people misuse a position as an excuse to hurt others, the problem is the person's perversion, not the position.

10. Throwing out words like *hater* distracts us from examining the issues, emphasizing unproductive attacks on character.

8

GAY CHRISTIANS

No evil dooms us hopelessly except the evil we love, and desire
to continue in, and make no effort to escape from.

—George Eliot

The idea of same-sex-attracted people coming to church is nothing new.

Paul wrote to Corinth around AD 53, pointing out that some of the Corinthian believers had been involved in homosexuality. Reminding them this was one of several sins excluding people from the kingdom, he brought it home: "And such were some of you" (1 Cor. 6:11).

Homosexuality was widely practiced in that region, so inevitably people who'd been involved in it heard the gospel, turned from immorality, and were now in communion with other believers. No question they had their struggles. It's easy to envision some in the early church feeling strong homosexual attractions, wrestling with them as with any sinful impulses, while moving ahead in grace and sanctification.

Or not. Human nature hasn't changed. It's also easy to envision some early believers giving up, tired of resisting desires that felt so natural, unwilling to persist in saying no to the flesh. So what we're facing in today's church is not unique. Christ's body has always included people who repented of homosexual behavior and faithfully stewarded their bodies to the end. But it has no doubt also included those who decided to indulge what they initially resisted.

What's new, though, is the growing approval of that decision by many Christian leaders and laity. Parts of the church now mirror the culture's shift toward acceptance of homosexuality, a trend some call progress, others call apostasy.

Regardless, the population identifying as "gay Christian" is growing, leaving us to wrestle with the oft-asked question, "Can someone really be both gay and Christian?"

Is There Such a Thing?

You can't answer the question without defining both terms.

Gay can refer to someone sexually active, whether in a relationship or more casual encounters. Or it can mean a person who's not sexually active but is willing if and when the time seems right. It can also refer to a Christian who believes homosexuality is wrong but is tempted that direction and sometimes yields. Yet again, it could mean someone who's homosexual in attraction only but chooses not to act on the attraction. Clearly the term's meaning influences the question's answer.

Now, *Christian,* for some, implies simply being "saved"; to others it implies both being saved and walking in rightness before God.

Muddying the waters further is the question of salvation. Can it be lost, or is it a once-and-for-all status? How you view eternal security will likewise direct your answer to the gay Christian question.

So let's do some semantic unpacking.

Though the question's settled for the Revisionist, for us who see homosexuality as sin, it's not so easily answered, since it raises the broader question: Can a Christian continually sin and remain a Christian? If so, and if *Christian* simply means "saved," then a gay Christian becomes possible. Suppose a homosexual person is truly born again, then relapses into unrepentant sin, even to the point of embracing a gay identity and claiming her behavior acceptable before God. She would still, according to the doctrine of eternal security, remain a Christian positionally ("saved") and would therefore be a gay Christian. But she'd also be a Christian outside God's will, for which she'll be chastened in this life (Heb. 12:7–11; Rev. 3:19) and at the judgment seat of Christ (2 Cor. 5:10).

Some who hold to eternal security might argue that, if she continues in sin, she was never really born again, an opinion bolstered by verses like 1 John 2:19, where John declared that certain apostates left the church because they were never true saints. But eternal security also stresses verses like John 10:28, where Jesus affirmed that no one can pluck His own from His hand. This would imply that a believer who sins remains a believer, no matter how egregious or continual the sin, so accordingly, a gay Christian remains a possibility.

For many, though, Paul's assertion in 1 Corinthians 6:9–10 that people indulging homosexually will not inherit the kingdom seems unqualified. Verses like that, along with Jesus's warning in John 15:6 (that believers not abiding in Him eventually wither and are burned), incline us to believe a Christian's ongoing sexual sin will at some point reap eternal judgment. So for those unconvinced of the once-saved-always-saved view, the term *gay Christian* is problematic.

We can, of course, recognize that God gives grace to erring Christians. Some believers occasionally indulge a temptation, confess, then perhaps relapse again. While there's no justification for such transgressions, most of us don't believe they nullify salvation. We rely on the 1 John 1:9 promise that God is faithful and just to forgive the sins we confess, and that He declines setting numerical limits on the transgressions He'll forgive (Ps. 32:1–2).

So a believer occasionally yielding to homosexual sin, yet confessing it as sin, remains a believer, and most of us are loathe to say that a first, second, or third transgression cancels out his salvation. I myself continued in homosexual sin as a believer for six years, and I'm inclined to view myself as backslidden during that time—saved, but deceived and seriously wrong.

So I find it useless to challenge a gay Christian's claim of salvation, because I cannot see into his soul; I can't accurately judge. Besides, a Christian can sin while remaining saved. Such a believer's eternity, and what it takes to jeopardize it, is open to debate.

After all, the believers in Corinth were carnal (1 Cor. 3:3), one of them incestuously coupling with his stepmother (5:1), yet they were all part of the local church community. Most of the churches in Revelation received serious correction from the Lord (Rev. 2–3), yet He referred to them as "the church." So can a person deliberately sin and still be a Christian? Hesitantly, I'd say yes.

I'd also say that's a dangerous, precarious path to walk, and if *Christian* should actually be narrowed to mean both saved and walking rightly before God, and if *gay* is defined to imply homosexual behavior, I couldn't with integrity say one could be both gay and Christian. To practice homosexuality is to behave outside clearly proscribed, God-given boundaries. That can't be right, and if *Christian* is limited by right living, then *gay* and *Christian* are incompatible.

That's why I also reject the term *gay Christian* when applied to someone who's repented of homosexuality, is homosexually tempted, and chooses to resist those temptations. While I celebrate the decision to live rightly, I question the appropriateness of adopting a seemingly positive label for sinful tendencies God calls us to resist rather than identify with.

I can appreciate someone saying, "I'm a Christian who deals with same-sex temptations"—an honest statement. But a believer claiming the "gay" label seems both an overidentification and a misidentification.

For all these reasons, I find it more useful to shift the discussion from whether a person embracing homosexuality can be saved, and instead focus on the more immediate issue: Can such a person be *right*?

The Growing Phenomenon

Self-identified "gay Christians" would answer yes. The population isn't new, but its visibility and increased credibility certainly are.

The earliest visible group seems to have been the Universal Fellowship of Metropolitan Community Churches (UFMCC), founded in Los Angeles in 1968 on the premise that homosexuality and Christianity are compatible.[1] The pro-gay Catholic group Dignity was formed the following year,[2] and in 1975 a group calling itself both evangelical and gay—Evangelicals Concerned—was birthed on the East Coast.[3] These organizations operated outside mainstream church life, unrecognized by any denomination, and disapproved of by virtually all churches for decades. They came to rely heavily on early pro-gay theological works, such as John Boswell's *Christianity, Social Tolerance, and Homosexuality*[4] and Letha Scanzoni and Virginia Mollenkott's *Is the Homosexual My Neighbor?*[5] for doctrinal support, but these books, like the groups, had limited exposure to the general Christian population.

So traditionally, within Bible-believing churches, a member with same-sex desires tended to believe she had only three options: resist the desires, indulge them secretly and then repent, or abandon the faith altogether. Indulging the desires openly, while identifying as gay and Christian, was unheard of.

But that fourth option became more prominent as the culture moved toward condoning homosexuality over the following decades, also embracing pro-gay theology and giving it visibility, emboldening those advocating its acceptance within their churches.

The results are impressive. As of 2016, while early groups like the UFMCC, Evangelicals Concerned, and Dignity still thrive, mainline denominations like the Evangelical Lutheran Church of America,[6] the Episcopal Church,[7] and the Presbyterian Church USA,[8] along with many independent gay-affirming churches, now join in openly supporting same-sex marriage and welcoming practicing homosexuals into membership. Pro-gay theology now enjoys support from high-profile leaders who identify as evangelicals, like Dr. Tony Campolo[9] and ethicist David Gushee,[10] as well as doctrinally liberal but influential leaders like Rob Bell.[11]

Modern support for the gay Christian position also comes from highly successful, now openly lesbian or gay Christian musicians like Vicky Beeching,[12] Ray Boltz,[13] Jennifer Knapp,[14] and gospel singer Anthony Williams.[15] Heterosexual allies, like the renowned contemporary Christian group Jars of Clay[16] and the former editor of *Contemporary Christian Music* magazine,[17] say amen to all of this, as does influential blogger Rachel Held Evans.[18]

WaterBrook Multnomah, a well-known and widely respected Christian publishing house, released Matthew Vines's pro-gay theological defense, *God and the Gay Christian,* in 2014, a decision leading to their resignation from the National Religious Broadcasters in light of the association's vociferous disapproval of the publication.[19] And support for anyone seeking harmony between their homosexuality and their faith can be found in popular online groups like the Gay Christian Network,[20] Gay Christian Online,[21] and Gays for Jesus.[22]

Consider all of this from the perspective of the believer who wrestles with same-sex temptations. Imagine you have sexual desires you never wanted and would erase if you could. On one hand, your local church condemns these desires as sinful, though it also offers you little or no supportive guidance. On the other hand, an abundance of supportive guidance from the pro-gay view is within reach. Mainline denominations approve of your desires. Respected evangelical leaders, some of whose books are in your church's library, are challenging your church's position, not your sexuality. Christian artists whose music you grew up absorbing are now out of the closet, claiming to have reconciled their sexuality and their faith. Mainline Christian publishers now produce books debunking all you've been taught about homosexuality. And a click of your mouse connects you with believers like yourself, who've made the shift from *This is my private struggle* to *This is my out-and-proud identity.*

Is there any reason for surprise when struggling Christians finally abandon the Traditional view and embrace the Revisionist one? Not only is this option convenient, but to the woman or man exhausted from a lonely battle, it's also a dead ringer for answered prayer.

Today's believer is likely to interact with someone saying, "I'm gay and Christian." Four general Revisionist arguments are likely to arise in that interaction:

1. Reinterpretation of Scripture (pro-gay theology)
2. Salvation status ("I'm gay, still saved, and confident")
3. Good fruit, good tree ("How can I bear good fruit if I'm wrong?")
4. Minimizing the difference ("Let's not divide over this non-essential issue")

Since chapters 9–13 will look in detail at argument 1, we'll focus in this chapter on the remaining three.

Traditional Position

Christians sin, so it's possible that someone may be gay and Christian, depending on your definition of the terms. But since homosexual acts occur outside God's design, they can't be justified, and the person committing them cannot be right. God therefore calls the same-sex-attracted Christian sometimes to marriage, sometimes to celibacy, but always to obedience.

REVISIONIST ARGUMENT 1

Salvation status: I'm gay, still saved, and confident.

This argument comes from someone who probably had a genuine rebirth experience, maybe evidenced by years of living as a committed believer. More often than not, he initially resisted his sexual feelings, then decided to stop fighting, and found that he still retained his basic doctrinal beliefs.

Moreover, genuine faith is often still evidenced in the person's life via love for worship, Scripture, prayer, and fellowship. Often the gay Christian adheres to orthodox theology, holding to the divinity of Christ, the authority of Scripture, and a generally sound approach to doctrine. So it becomes easier to think, "Hey, I accepted my sexuality and everything's still in place. What's the problem?"

I can't count the number of times I've heard, "I've really prayed about this. I've sought God, and I feel confident He's fine with where I am as a gay Christian." How do you argue with someone's confidence before God?

FIRST RESPONSE: **The rightness of homosexuality, not your salvation, is being challenged.**

The Traditionalist is not trying to second-guess the gay Christian's spiritual status but is challenging the notion that simply being saved legitimizes a behavior.

Clearly there's a difference between being saved and being right. Peter was saved, yet wrong when he distanced himself from Gentiles in fear of Jewish disapproval (Gal. 2:11–16). Corinthian believers were called "saints" (1 Cor. 1:2), yet were wrong when they took each other to court (6:1–8), got drunk at the Lord's Supper (11:20–21), separated into factions (3:4), and were proud of their tolerance for lewdness (5:1–6). Surely they couldn't claim their salvation was proof of right behavior because, in the end, "saved" doesn't mean "right."

SECOND RESPONSE: **If your ongoing behavior is clearly outside biblical guidelines, you should reexamine your relationship with Christ.**

A believer may be in no position to judge the spiritual status of another believer, but he is in a position to encourage that believer to reexamine his or her own status.

Paul did just that when he asked the Corinthians to "examine yourselves as to whether you are in the faith. Test yourselves" (2 Cor. 13:5). There's likewise a place for Christians to admonish ("warn" or "exhort") each other, something Paul called us to do in four different letters (Rom. 15:14; Col. 3:16; 1 Thess. 5:14; and 2 Thess. 3:15). After all, anyone can say, "I love God." The proof of love for Him lies in obedience to what He's revealed.

Empathizing with another's experience is helpful, but it's necessary at times to go further, because John's statement in 1 John 3:9—"Whoever has been born of God does not sin, for His seed remains in him; and he cannot sin, because he has been born of God"—should arouse our concern for anyone continuing to practice blatant sin. Obviously John wasn't describing true believers as sinless. But as Mike Oppenheimer, founder of Let Us Reason Ministries, writes,

> "Cannot sin" means one who is born again does not CON-TINUALLY sin, as he once did or is not HABITUALLY a sinner as he was before he came to know Jesus. There is a difference, as light has come to rule over the darkness. The born again believer has no compulsion to do sin over and over as he once had been driven by his fallen nature. If a man continually and habitually sins, it may prove that he has NEVER been renewed.[23]

To be saved means to have a new nature that cannot indefinitely coexist restfully with habitual sin. Or, as Martin Luther noted, "The child of God in this conflict receives indeed wounds daily, but never throws away his arms or makes peace with his deadly foe."[24]

If this is true, then one who claims to be a Christian but continually practices unbiblical behavior raises legitimate concerns, no matter how commonly accepted the behavior or how controversial to confront it. So to the person claiming to be gay and Christian, the Traditionalist might ask, lovingly but to the point, "Are you sure?"

THIRD RESPONSE: **Confidence in experience over sound doctrine is a poor foundation.**

When my father was diagnosed with throat cancer in 1988, my wife and I immediately prayed for his healing. I felt God's presence, His peace, and the wonderful sense of His voice calming me, promising, "I love you, I love your dad, and I'm taking care of all this."

I took that to mean Dad would be fine. And why not? I'd just married, our family ties were better than ever, and losing him was unthinkable. I was wrong. God's reassurance wasn't in fact the answer I assumed, and Dad left us within months. The strength of my hope that God would say yes had been all too easy to mistake for an actual yes.

My confidence was real. But it was grounded in the wrong source.

So with feelings. When we judge something's rightness or wrongness primarily by our conscience, confidence, peace, or whatever experiential device we lean on, we're taking advice from the wrong source. At our best, we have a boundless capacity to kid ourselves. (See Jer. 17:9, where the heart is described as "deceitful above all things.") We may want to do God's will but still have strong desires to do our own, coupled with an earnest hope that ours and His are the same.

The best of us is subject to imposing our preferred answer onto God, and the more important the issue, the deeper this inclination. Which is exactly why we've been given a written, sure foundation in the Scriptures. David described them as a guiding lamp (Ps. 119:105) to rely on for personal moral cleansing (119:9). Hebrews says they override our ideas and intentions (Heb. 4:12), and Paul said they provide "instruction in righteousness" (2 Tim. 3:16).

God's Word is an objective certainty, in clear contrast to my longings, and my inclination to believe my desires are His promises.

That said, we can and should appreciate how hard it is for a Christian to deal with homosexuality and the myriad complications that come with it. We can also appreciate how a gay Christian—tired of the struggle, of being misunderstood, of saying no to what seems so normal—could hope so strongly that homosexuality is OK with God that he would misinterpret his hope as God's yes.

Adding to the confusion may be the Holy Spirit's inward witness that the gay Christian is loved, valued, and precious in God's sight. How easily we can mistake, as I did, God's reassurance of our value as permission to move in the direction we want to go!

Yet "I love you, My child" can hardly be equated with "You have My permission." Permission denied in Scripture will always be permission denied in fact.

So my confidence levels or conscience matter only somewhat. But what the Word plainly states matters hugely. Only when the Bible provides no specific guidance can we defer to conscience as a guiding principle. Otherwise, when it comes to determining what's right versus wrong, the key question must always be Paul's: "What does the Scripture say?" (Rom. 4:3).

Good person, right position: How can I bear good fruit in my life if I'm wrong?

When someone's personality, character, and gifting are all good, it's easy to believe those three elements prove his position is right. It's also a mistake.

But an understandable mistake, especially regarding this issue. I've often thought, in the years since I left the gay church and community, that if likableness alone proved sound doctrine, then gay Christians would be among the most theologically solid people alive. Many that I knew were more biblically literate than a high percentage of Traditionalists. And the ones I was closest to were also warm, clever, loyal, devout, and sincere.

Gifted, too, with endowments I believe were genuine spiritual giftings. When I first joined the Metropolitan Community Church in Southern California in 1978, I found teachers gifted in exposition, evangelists who boldly proclaimed a plain gospel message to nonbelieving gays and lesbians, and intercessors skilled in deep, disciplined prayer.

One Halloween evening, for example, my partner and I joined our lesbian pastor and her partner for a night of intercessory prayer for kids' safety, and against dark forces. An ordained lesbian, her lover, and two gay men spent that evening on our knees doing battle against spiritual wickedness. That's typical of the complications you discover when you examine gay Christians' life experiences. Which led me to believe that bad trees couldn't possibly produce such good fruit, which is still a common, and wrong, conclusion.

Christian blogger Rachel Held Evans describes her participation in the Gay Christian Network conference as "a Christian conference so energized by the Spirit, so devoid of empty showmanship or preoccupation with image, so grounded in love and abounding in grace." Calling the gathering "Church if I've ever experienced it," she concludes, "I'm convinced LGBT Christians have a special role to play in teaching the Church what it means to be Christian."[25]

Admiration for their good qualities also seems to have played a role in Dr. Tony Campolo's conversion from Traditionalist to Revisionist stance:

> "One reason I am changing my position on this issue is that, through Peggy," said Campolo of his wife, Peggy, "I have come to know so many gay Christian couples whose relationships work in much the same way as our own. Our friendships with these couples have helped me understand how important it is for the exclusion and disapproval of their unions by the Christian community to end. We in the Church should actively support such families."[26]

Highly respected Christian ethicist and professor David Gushee describes a similar epiphany while getting to know gay Christians: "It is hard to describe exactly why my moral vision shifted in this way. But undoubtedly, it had much to do with my move to Atlanta in 2007 and my growing contact with LGBT people, especially fellow Christians. I hardly knew anyone who was gay before that move, but afterward, they seemed to be everywhere, and a few became very dear friends."[27]

But if sensing the Spirit's presence, or appreciating the character or personality of gay Christians, can convince a sympathetic heterosexual that the gay Christian position is valid, imagine the power it can have on the Christian who's personally navigating the sexual and spiritual journey.

FIRST RESPONSE: **Good gifts don't validate bad doctrine.**

Some would write off these folks "sensing the Spirit" as emotionalism or delusion, and it may have been.

But not necessarily. Evidently the Holy Spirit's manifestation in the Corinthian church was significant enough for Paul to write at length about the proper exercise of spiritual gifts (1 Cor. 12 and 14). Regardless of your position on such gifts today, clearly they were evidence of the Holy Spirit's ministry in that situation. The relevant point is that gifts were evidenced among people who were seriously wrong.

We're all aware of past sexual scandals among well-known pastors, televangelists, or Christian artists. Yet in hindsight we note that, even when these ministers practiced ongoing immorality, their ministerial gifts remained intact. The gifts couldn't justify the sin, nor did the sin nullify the gifts.

All of which reminds us, "The gifts and the calling of God are irrevocable" (Rom. 11:29). The manifestation of God's presence is ultimately a display of grace, not a reward for good works, nor proof of right teaching, nor a seal of approval for behavior.

SECOND RESPONSE: **Good people do bad things.**

Honest, giving, warmhearted, charismatic people can also be wrong, seriously compromised, even deceived. It's wrong to assume that someone who's good must also be right.

And it's just as wrong to assume that someone in serious error must also have a repulsive personality and low character. Christians today are, in my opinion, subject to both extremes. Which is needless, because we can recognize a person's good qualities and their error simultaneously, one not canceling the other.

Good people can do bad things. Look no further than King David, the man after God's heart, who gave himself permission to murder an innocent man so his adultery wouldn't be exposed (2 Sam. 11).

Gay Christians can be likable and in many ways people of good character. Look no further than those you are likely to encounter. And while their error cannot nullify their good qualities, neither can those qualities nullify the severity of their error.

REVISIONIST ARGUMENT 3

Minimizing the difference: Let's not
divide over this nonessential issue.

The goal of a Revisionist talking with you is usually *your conversion*. If he has revised his understanding of Scripture, he'll hope to persuade you to do the same. He feels the issue is important, and that your Traditional viewpoint is not only wrong but damaging (see chap. 7).

But since you may not change your position, his next best goal is *minimization*. If you persist in your position, maybe you'll come to see it as a nonessential issue, as we view other secondary doctrinal issues. For instance, we may hold clear positions on whether the rapture will be pre-, mid-, or post-tribulation, but seldom do we hear of Christians breaking fellowship over it. We generally see this as a doctrinal fine point we can "agree to disagree" on, and rightly so.

If we view homosexuality in the same light, then gay Christians and Traditionalists can rise above just being good neighbors in peaceful coexistence (a goal I hope we can all agree on). They can also commune as fellow believers, worshiping together in the same churches, and shrugging off their differences as minor and not worth dividing over.

This may look good on paper. Getting along is preferable whenever possible, as Paul enjoined: "As much as depends on you, live peaceably with all men" (Rom. 12:18) while "endeavoring to keep the unity of the Spirit in the bond of peace" (Eph. 4:3). It's preferable not to divide; in most cases it's also right.

FIRST RESPONSE: **When confrontation is called for, communion is sin.**

Yet getting along isn't primary. When "unity" takes precedence over truth, then we've morphed from unity to enabling, appeasing the sin we should be opposing. Pastor Adrian Rogers said, "It is better to be divided by truth than to be united in error."[28]

That division shouldn't come easily. Believers aren't intended to nitpick each other, sniffing out flaws and appointing ourselves judges. Our love for the brethren calls us to build each other up, patiently bearing with each other's weaknesses.

But some behaviors indicate overt rebellion, not just weaknesses, and call for confrontation and sometimes church discipline.

So when Paul learned the believers in Corinth were approving of incest, he seemed angrier at the church community than at the sinning man. He rebuked them for pride in their tolerance, reminding them that serious sin tolerated in the congregation infects the whole body (1 Cor. 5:6–8) and that we should have no association with believers practicing sexual sin, idolatry, greed, violence, drunkenness, or swindling (5:11–13). It's easy to guess what Paul would say to minimizing homosexuality within the church in the interest of unity.

Breaking fellowship is certainly a last resort when someone refuses to repent of serious wrongdoing, but Paul told the Thessalonians to note and avoid anyone defying the instructions he'd written (2 Thess. 3:14), and he commanded withdrawing from idle, disruptive, or rebellious Christians (3:6–12). Seem harsh? It is.

But suppose a member of your local church was an avowed racist. Suppose he sported swastika tattoos on his arms, easily viewed when he lifted his hands in praise. Then in the fellowship hall after service, he openly admitted to hating African Americans, Hispanics, and Jews.

Where's your tolerance now? I should hope you'd insist the church leadership confront him, trying to persuade him of the biblical viewpoint on race and our inherent equality in God's sight. And, should he persist, you'd expect leadership to disfellowship him as a last resort, after several attempts at persuasion, to prevent his offending and infecting the congregation with his ideas and behavior.

Now here's the rub: There are different *types* of serious wrongdoing, but all serious wrongdoing should still be dealt with.

As a staunch Traditionalist, I'll be the first to say I wouldn't react as viscerally toward a gay Christian in my church as I would toward an avowed racist. But sexual sin, while not evoking the same emotions as racism, is still categorized as severe—severe enough to warrant confrontation when needed. Paul's warning that "a little leaven leavens the whole lump" (1 Cor. 5:6) was valid and practical. If we tolerate something we're called to forbid, we invite toleration of more and worse.

Tolerating practice of one sexual sin within the church encourages members to be less watchful of their own lusts and to more readily indulge them. Parents can hardly expect their teens to take biblical admonitions against fornication seriously when their church doesn't take the biblical male-female requirement for marital union both literally and seriously.

And if we tolerate revision of Scripture on something as basic as the definition of family, we encourage other revisions of equally important doctrines whenever revisions seem convenient or appealing. Then those who understandably recoil at the thought of hell, or the notion that there's no way to the Father but by Christ, will more readily revise the offensive Scriptures, because they've already seen it done and accepted in their church.

If we minimize the seriousness of stepping outside clearly defined standards for sexual behavior, we encourage a similarly cavalier attitude toward stepping outside clearly defined standards for other behaviors as well. Then you can expect the person tempted toward overt greed, or dishonesty, or selfishness to give herself permission to violate the respective biblical prohibitions. After all, she's seen others in her congregation do the same with impunity.

What we tolerate, we will also in some way come to emulate.

Second Response: **Minimization moves us toward Revision.**

In 2004 Tony Campolo wrote in his book *Speaking My Mind* that, while he held the Traditional view on homosexuality, he didn't see it as an essential doctrinal or moral issue, and therefore it was nothing to divide over.[29] Today his shift to a solidly Revisionist view is well known.[30]

Chuck Smith Jr., son of renowned Bible teacher Chuck Smith, founder of the Calvary Chapel movement, declared in 2004 that he was "rethinking" his Traditionalist stance on homosexuality, largely because of his interactions with gay Christians.[31] Within five years he was openly affirming same-sex unions and advocating as a Revisionist.[32]

In 2006 popular author and speaker Brian McLaren called for a five-year pastoral moratorium on taking clear positions on homosexuality, allowing church leaders to consider what theologians, geneticists, sociologists, psychologists, and ethicists had to say.[33] Six years later he plainly stated that, while he used to take the Scriptures condemning homosexuality at face value, he now realized he'd been "wrong on this issue" and had joined the Revisionist ranks.[34]

Minimizing the seriousness of doctrines leads to the dismantling of those doctrines, and the general acceptance of that dismantling.

So when denominations like the Presbyterian Church USA, the Evangelical Lutheran Church of America, and the Episcopal Church shifted to gay-affirming official positions, they didn't do so overnight. They first allowed prohomosexual groups to form within their denominations, despite the groups' adherence to views contradicting the official church stances. It was as if the denominations were saying, "We believe and practice *This*, but if you believe and practice *That*, we'll allow you to continue in fellowship with us for unity's sake."

Inevitably, with time and patient effort by Revisionists, *This* came to be officially revised to *That*. Which is why, to my thinking, Christian universities, Bible colleges, or denominations allowing pro-gay groups to organize under their umbrellas are simply kidding themselves, in denial that such organizing will lead to official revision.

Judge not: Saying homosexuality is a sin means you're judging!

Jesus's admonition not to judge (Matt. 7:1–3) is often invoked to discourage Traditionalists from stating their position, much less having their churches adhere to it. In fact, "Judge not" may now be one of Jesus's most oft-quoted phrases.

FIRST RESPONSE: **Jesus did not say we can't make judgments and, in fact, commanded us to do just that.**

Taking the entire passage in context, Jesus didn't say, "Never judge," but rather He warned that if we judge, the same standard we apply to others will be applied to us (7:2) and that it's a sin of hypocrisy to judge another person's fault without first examining our own (7:3). When comparing Scripture to Scripture, we find Jesus was not prohibiting all judgments, because He gave us too many commands that require us to judge.

He said to rebuke a brother who sins against you (18:15), requiring you to make a judgment call about another person's sin. He also enjoined us to "judge with righteous judgment" (John 7:24) and to evaluate the fruit another person bears, which requires judging (Matt. 7:16). And He quite publicly judged scribes and Pharisees (23:13), contradicting Himself if all forms of judgment are sinful.

Likewise, Paul rebuked the Corinthians for *not* judging the behavior of a man (1 Cor. 5:1–3); lamented that they had no one willing to make judgments in disputes (6:2–5); and told Timothy to "convince, rebuke, exhort" (2 Tim. 4:2), all of which require judging.

<u>Second Response:</u> **It's impossible not to judge.**

Everyone, regardless of their belief system, believes some things are right and others wrong. So to assume we're not to judge is also to assume we're somehow to suspend all sense of moral structure.

"Whoever Tells the Best Stories Wins"

Stories often trump bare, boring facts in this age of narrative over analysis. Rather than think critical issues through, many of us simply absorb the stories of the people involved and make decisions based on which narrative gained our sympathy and support.

To my thinking, that's a sloppy foundation for distinguishing right from wrong. But it's prevalent.

Still, stories are compelling. After considering the merits of an argument, it helps to hear people's stories from both sides of the issue. So while I disagree with gay Christians' conclusions, I'd say their stories are necessary to hear. They remind us that many within the church experience same-sex attractions, sitting in our pews silent and afraid. While many churches now offer ministries to alcoholics, drug addicts, and the financially irresponsible who want to correct their behaviors, little is offered to the same-sex struggler.

These stories also remind us that such strugglers often endure the slings and arrows of fellow believers who make crass jokes about homosexuals without realizing whom they may be wounding. And they remind us of the profound grief in facing the possibility of life without sexual fulfillment if what would fulfill you most is forbidden and difficult even to discuss. We can glean all of this from the stories of those identifying as gay Christians.

But such stories should nudge us toward improving, not revising, our position. If we've said we love the sinner but hate the sin, and later realized we've done the love part less effectively than we could have, then surely leaping to love *for the sin* is reckless. Love for the sinner cannot necessitate encouraging behavior that is, in the end, surely detrimental to his best interest.

Which is a point I've personally come to appreciate. When I repented of homosexuality, I did it initially out of obedience to God, nothing more. I knew I was outside His will, a place I was no longer willing to park.

Only recently, after thirty-plus years, have I come to realize that what I thought I was doing for God was also in my own best interest, opening up aspects of life and joy I'd never have experienced otherwise. I'm sure this is why C. S. Lewis noted, "When we want to be something other than the thing God wants us to be, we must be wanting what, in fact, will not make us happy."[35]

Thus Paul Morris poses one of the most relevant questions for someone attempting to harmonize sound doctrine with homosexuality, a question worth repeating when discussing truth with a gay Christian: "If I were a Christian homosexual, I think this one question would disturb me most: Am I trying to interpret scripture in light of my proclivity, or should I interpret my proclivity in light of scripture?"[36]

Ten Talking Points about Gay Christians

1. A Christian can be both saved and wrong; the one does not cancel the other.

2. Believers can and do bear bad fruit, as numerous biblical examples prove.

3. The church of Corinth condoned a man living in an incestuous relationship. Paul did not suggest that Christianity justified this behavior, nor that this behavior negated their Christianity.

4. We don't decide which desires to indulge simply by their persistence or duration. We let the Word guide us.

5. The gay Christian usually doesn't make the decision to "default" to homosexual attractions *after* careful study of Scripture, but *before*. He decides to embrace the behavior, then finds a way to biblically justify what he's embraced.

6. If my sinful tendencies aren't removed despite my prayers, then God is giving me a commission, not permission. I'm commissioned to steward my sexuality, not given permission to indulge it as I see fit.

7. Anyone can say, "I love God." The proof of love for Him lies in obedience to what He's revealed.

8. People in error can experience the Holy Spirit's manifestation in their lives.

9. If your behavior disqualifies you from fellowship, the church has no choice but to recognize that and act accordingly.

10. To continue in a sin that Scripture plainly says disqualifies you from the kingdom is a dangerous, possibly eternally fatal error.

9

SODOM

Oh, this was the great ploy of Satan in that kingdom of his: to display such blatant evil one could almost believe one's own secret sin didn't matter.

—Corrie Ten Boom, *The Hiding Place*

Sodom was notoriously evil, a point on which everyone agrees. Arguments flare when Sodom's evil is assumed to be homosexuality, so the story of Sodom's destruction is relevant to us and likely to arise in conversation.

When Abraham and his nephew, Lot, parted company, Lot noticed the well-watered plains of the Jordan and decided to relocate his family to Sodom, a part of that region (Gen. 13:10–12). The first description of its inhabitants describes them as "exceedingly wicked and sinful against the LORD" (13:13), so God informed Abraham He intended to destroy it (18:20–23). Afraid for Lot and his family, Abraham bargained with God to spare the city if a certain number of righteous people might be found in it (18:23–32). God agreed to withhold judgment if ten righteous Sodomites existed.

Genesis 19:1–11 proves they didn't. Two angels approached Lot's home, where at sundown all the city's men descended, demanding Lot release his guests to be gang-raped. Lot offered his daughters instead, but the Sodomites persisted, and the angels ushered Lot and his family away just before God decimated Sodom with fire (19:12–24).

Subsequently throughout the Bible, Sodom is referred to twenty-seven times as an example of wickedness and divine judgment, and the term *sodomite* eventually came to be associated with homosexuality.

Traditional Position

Homosexuality, though not the only sin of Sodom, was widespread. All the city's men coming out to participate in male-on-male rape indicates this, as do Ezekiel's references to Sodomite abominations (Ezek. 16:50), Peter's reference to their "filthy conduct" (2 Pet. 2:6–7), and Jude's reference to their fornication (Jude 7). Therefore, God's destruction of a city widely practicing homosexuality, among other sins, is an indictment against homosexuality itself.

Because this account includes many repellent behaviors—attempted gang rape, offering one's daughters to appease, drunken father-daughter intercourse in the aftermath—Revisionists often dismiss it as irrelevant to discussions on homosexuality. Since the homosexual behavior described was violent, not consensual, they claim it has nothing to do with consensual same-sex relations. The Revisionist approach to Sodom rests on three arguments:

Sodom's sin was inhospitality, not homosexuality.

Boswell claims this,[1] as do Vines,[2] Scroggs,[3] Gay Christian 101,[4] Religious Tolerance,[5] and John McNeil.[6] All of them stress that inhospitality was considered a serious offense in that culture. Violating guests was a breach of hospitality codes, and an invitation to wrath.

Vines quotes subsequent verses associating Sodom with inhospitality (Matt. 10:14–15; Luke 10:10–12) and concludes, "The men were their guests, and the 'sacred duty of hospitality' . . . was paramount."[7]

Boswell suggests Sodom's men were outraged that Lot, himself a foreigner, had brought strangers within city limits. Fearing potential invasion, they became abusive. He cites Deuteronomy 23:3–4, condemning Ammon's inhospitality toward Israel, then concludes, "In nearly all such stories evil persons appear either as neighbors or other townsfolk who do not fulfill their obligation and are punished."[8] In other words, God destroyed Sodom for inhospitality, even to foreigners.

FIRST RESPONSE: **Sodom's sin preexisted the angels' visit.**

This argument, like other Revisionist approaches to Sodom, makes too much of what happened in Genesis 19 and too little of what happened beforehand.

Sodom was under judgment before the angels visited. God told Abraham He intended to destroy the city, whose wickedness "cried out" before Him (18:20–21). So the fire was already going to fall, and the angels' mistreatment, while unspeakable, only sealed an established fate.

SECOND RESPONSE: **This approach is too limiting.**

It's possible that such mistreatment of strangers happened regularly there, which no doubt played into the scenario. But that would be a minor part of the broader evil for which God condemned Sodom. Sodom's inhospitality is undeniable. But sexual violence (19:4–11), indifference to the poor (Ezek. 16:49), and lasciviousness (Jude 7) are some of the other sins also contributing to its downfall. Narrowing the list to inhospitality seriously underestimates Sodom's moral stench.

REVISIONIST ARGUMENT 2

Sodom's sin was attempted rape, not homosexuality.

Gushee agrees with the "inhospitality" interpretation, but also stresses the story's violent aspects as evidence it condemns attempted rape and humiliation, not homosexuality.[9] He considers this horrendous, not only for the violence of rape, but for the additional humiliation inflicted on a male rape victim. According to this view, one man's sexual subjugation over another imposed severe shame, leaving the "conquering" rapist powerful and the "conquered" subject powerless and demeaned.

Prison rape is a modern parallel. The rapist is generally less interested in sex, more interested in enhancing his own power at the expense of the victim's. It's a despicable but effective way of saying, "I'm in charge," a sentiment probably underlying every act of sexual violence.

But rape hardly describes routine sexual unions between men; indeed, this story is completely disconnected from the average homosexual relationship or encounter. So, the argument assumes, Sodom's sin wasn't same-sex relations, but attempting cruel violations, leaving a man physically abused and emotionally shattered.

Response: Where homosexual rape is practiced, homosexual acts are probably common.
No Traditionalist would suggest the rapists of Sodom represented most homosexuals, any more than we'd suggest male-on-male rape represents most male-to-male sex. The event recorded in Genesis 19 is as far removed from common homosexual relations as the rape of the concubine in Judges 19:22–25 is removed from common heterosexual relations.

But that doesn't make the story irrelevant, nor does it erase homosexuality from Sodom's landscape.

Note that all men of the city, young and old, turned out for this assault. Whether they all intended to participate, or only some while others watched, it reveals a common desire to engage in forced sex between men. And while it's possible all Sodom's males simply relished the idea of subjugating strangers, or were just curious observers, such a turnout implies the common practice of homosexuality.

Three specific references to the sexual nature of Sodom's sins bolster this point. Ezekiel 16:50 says of Sodom, "They were haughty and committed abominations before Me," using the same Hebrew word for "abomination"—*tō'ēvāh* (toh-ay-VAH)—that Leviticus 18:22 and 20:13 use to describe sex between men as "abomination."

Second Peter 2:6–7 mentions the "filthy conduct" of Sodom, using the word *aselgeia* (ah-SEL-gay-ah), found eight other times in the New Testament, and always, without exception, in the context of sexual sin. (Common English translations of *aselgeia* are "lasciviousness," "wantonness," "debauchery," and "lewdness.")

And Jude 7 describes Sodomites as "having given themselves over to sexual immorality and gone after strange flesh." "Sexual immorality" is clear, from the word *ekporneuō* (ek-por-NEW-oh), found only here in the New Testament (but related to the frequent word *porneuō*, from which we get *pornography*) and meaning "giving oneself to fornication."

But "strange flesh" is unclear. "Strange," from *heteros* (HEH-ter-oss), means "other" or "different"; "flesh," from *sarx* (sounds like it looks), refers to flesh of the physical body. But Revisionists like Vines[10] and Traditionalists like Robert Gagnon[11] agree it may well refer to humans sexually pursuing angels (which, in fact, the Sodomites unwittingly did).

Regardless, three facts are clear in Scripture:

- All of Sodom's men tried to engage in or support a forced homosexual act.
- The "abominations" practiced in Sodom are described by the same term referencing homosexuality elsewhere.
- Sexual immorality was widely practiced there.

These facts, combined, make it harder to believe homosexuality was *not* widespread in Sodom than to believe it was.

REVISIONIST ARGUMENT 3

The request to "know" the angels wasn't sexual, but only a request to "get to know" who they were.

Boswell and Bailey support this argument, based on the Hebrew word *yāda'* (yah-DAH), "to know." Boswell asserts that the word is rarely used in a sexual sense in the Old Testament,[12] and Bailey points out that the Septuagint Greek translation of *yāda'* in this verse means simply "making acquaintance of."[13] Therefore, they argue, the men just wanted to know who the visitors were, probably concerned about foreigners in their city, and implied no sexual intentions.

This is the weakest Revisionist argument regarding Sodom because it so blatantly contradicts the story's obvious elements.

FIRST RESPONSE: **This argument renders Lot's response nonsensical.**

Lot was extremely alarmed at the men's request, beseeching them not to "do so wickedly" (Gen. 19:7). He offered his daughters to use "as you wish" but pleaded that they "do nothing to these men" (19:8). That's an absurd, wild response to men just wanting to learn about his guests. Calling their intentions wicked, then offering his daughters (his emphasis on their virginity clearly implying sexual intent), confirms he was trying to prevent sexual violence, not a get-acquainted meeting.

SECOND RESPONSE: *Yāda'* **can have sexual implications.**

While *yāda'* usually refers to mental knowledge, Bailey's claim that it's used "rarely" sexually is understated. Genesis alone uses it six times specifically and undeniably referring to intercourse, including references to Adam and Cain "knowing" their wives (4:1, 17, 25), to Rebekah's virginity (24:16), and quite relevantly, to Lot's daughters' virginity, only three verses after the Sodomites' demand (19:8).

The fact the men used *yāda'* for their desire and the fact Lot replied using the same term for his daughters' virginity make it plain that the conversation's context, and therefore the meaning of *yāda'*, were both sexual.

So Was Sodom Destroyed Because of Homosexuality?

Traditionalists generally don't rely on Genesis 19 as the definitive objection to homosexuality, recognizing, with Revisionists, that the Sodom account doesn't provide a comprehensive argument. Thomas Schmidt observes, "The original offenders in Sodom . . . probably did not have what today we might call a homosexual orientation; rather, they attempted male rape as a means to humiliate."[14] And Gagnon writes, "To the extent that the story does not deal with consensual homosexual relationships, it is not an 'ideal' text to guide contemporary Christian sexual ethics."[15]

But both agree that the story is still relevant to our discussion. Schmidt mentions other sources equating Sodom with sexual sin or perversion, including the second-century *Testament of the Twelve Patriarchs*, labeling Sodomites "sexually promiscuous"; the *Testament of Benjamin*, saying Sodom "departed from the order of nature"; *Jubilees*, describing Sodomites "polluting themselves and fornicating in their flesh"; and both Philo and Josephus declaring "same-sex relations as the characteristic vice of Sodom."[16]

Gagnon adds,

The perversion of same-sex male intercourse appears to be an integral part of this story, along with other factors. Just as one form of illicit copulation (between angels and women) contributed to the earlier cataclysm of the great flood in Genesis 6 . . . so too another form of unnatural sexual relations (between men) served as a *key contributing factor* in the cataclysmic destruction of Sodom and Gomorrah.[17]

"A key contributing factor"—certainly not Sodom's only vice, certainly neither a minor one. Scripture's general testimony regarding this city is that it was extraordinarily wicked (Gen. 13:13), characterized by abomination (Ezek. 16:50) and specific sexual sins (2 Pet. 2:6–7 and Jude 7). Its citizens were prideful and idle, materially rich but indifferent to the poor (Ezek. 16:49), and their name is synonymous with debauchery.

To say Sodom was destroyed for homosexuality is an overstatement, as is the charge that homosexuality was the primary sin warranting God's wrath. But it's just as inaccurate to say homosexuality didn't figure into Sodom's profile, when, in fact, it seems to have figured largely.

Apologist Greg Koukl, analyzing Revisionist interpretations of Genesis 19, summarizes,

> Clearly, the general wickedness of Sodom and Gomorrah was great. That's not in question. Our concern here is whether homosexuality was part of that wickedness. Our analysis of Genesis shows that homosexuality was the principle behavior at issue in that passage. Ezekiel simply enumerates additional sins. The prophet doesn't contradict Moses, but rather gives more detail.
>
> Stinginess and arrogance alone did not draw God's wrath. Ezekiel anchored the list of crimes with the word "abominations." This word takes us right back to homosexuality.[18]

Ten Talking Points about Sodom

1. Inhospitality toward Lot's guests couldn't have been the reason for Sodom's destruction; before that visit, God intended to destroy the city.

2. The attempted rape of the angels was a symptom of the broader evil in Sodom, which had earned God's judgment long before the attempt.

3. The turnout of all the city's men for the attempted rape indicates homosexuality was widely practiced.

4. Ezekiel, Peter, and Jude all refer to the sexual nature of Sodom's sins.

5. The Sodomites' demand to "know" Lot's guests couldn't have been a request merely to learn about them. Lot's response proves their intentions were both evil and sexual.

6. Genesis uses *yāda'*, "to know," just as the Sodomites and Lot did—with specific sexual meaning. This sexual context clearly implies sexual content in the word.

7. Sodom was not destroyed over homosexuality alone; they displayed many critical sins.

8. Genesis 19 portrays homosexuality as outstanding evidence of Sodom's broader wickedness, a wickedness including, but also transcending, same-sex behavior (as we will also see in Rom. 1).

9. Traditionalists don't view the Sodom account as their prime supporting evidence, but as significant in portraying homosexuality as one of many Sodomite wrongs.

10. The sexual nature of the men's intentions, Ezekiel's application of "abomination" to Sodom, and the two New Testament references to Sodom's sexual sins all testify to sexual perversion as prominent in Sodom's profile.

10

HOMOSEXUALITY AND LEVITICUS

There is no point on which men make a greater mistake than
on the relation which exists between the law and the gospel.

—Charles Spurgeon

Back in 2000, an episode of the *West Wing* portrayed America's
president humiliating a conservative woman who cited Leviticus
to support her antihomosexual views. In rapid-fire style he cut
her down:

I wanted to ask you a couple of questions while I have you here.
I wanted to sell my youngest daughter into slavery, as sanctioned
in Exodus 21:7. What would be a good place for her to be? My
chief of staff insists on working on the Sabbath. Exodus 35:2
clearly says he should be stoned to death. Am I morally obliged
to kill him myself, or is it OK to call the police? Here's one
that's really important because we've got a lot of sports fans in
this town. Touching the skin of a dead pig makes one unclean,
according to Leviticus 11:7. If they promise to wear gloves, can
the Washington Redskins still play football?[1]

When a major television series shows the president slamming a religious conservative with a Revisionist argument, then the argument has obviously gained credence. (Browse the internet; you'll see the *West Wing* speech repeated frequently.) Clearly our traditional understanding of Leviticus is under fire.

Traditional Position

The theme of Leviticus is summed up in 11:45: "For I am the LORD who brings you up out of the land of Egypt, to be your God. You shall therefore be holy, for I am holy." The essence of holiness is separateness or differentness from all things worldly. Leviticus details the laws and ceremonies that Israel was to observe in living out their separation to God.

Twenty-seven chapters cover regulations for diet, the priesthood, sacrifices, hygiene, holy days, and civil and family relationships. Chapters 18 and 20 largely concern themselves with sexual behaviors. Chapter 18 forbids five: incest, intercourse during menstruation, adultery, homosexuality, and bestiality. Chapter 20 reiterates these prohibitions, commanding death sentences for anyone violating them, except for those regarding menstruation. It also cites cultic practices, idol worship, and cursing a parent.

The verses regarding homosexuality read,

- "You shall not lie with a male as with a woman. It is an abomination" (18:22).
- "If a man lies with a male as he lies with a woman, both of them have committed an abomination. They shall surely be put to death. Their blood shall be upon them" (20:13).

The Traditional position is that prohibitions against homosexuality, adultery, incest, and bestiality are applicable to ancient Israel and modern believers alike, because they are universal moral laws—not ritual laws specific to Israel—and they're reiterated throughout the Bible.

REVISIONIST ARGUMENT 1

Hypocrisy: You pick and choose which verses you take seriously.

This is the commonest rebuttal. Early Revisionists Tom Horner[2] and Troy Perry[3] proposed it, *The West Wing* employed it, a celebrity-studded 2008 video musicalized it,[4] and though Vines dismisses it,[5] you'll find it frequently recycled in blogs and conversations.

Supporters of this argument point out that Leviticus commands stoning homosexuals to death (20:13) and condemns wearing mixed fabric (19:19) and eating pigs (11:7) or shellfish (11:12). Then there's 18:19, forbidding sex during a woman's menstruation. So if you're against homosexuality because Leviticus condemns it, then to be consistent, you also must support and enforce all of the above and obey all other Levitical laws, imposing the penalties prescribed for those who break them. Which no one does.

Therefore, the argument concludes, positions based on Leviticus constitute hypocrisy.

FIRST RESPONSE: **Prohibitions against homosexuality transcend the Law of Moses.**

The relationship of Old Testament law to Christians is easily misunderstood. On one hand, the New Testament clearly describes certain Old Testament commands as nonbinding to Christians. (See, for example, Acts 10; 15:1–31; Col. 2:16–17.) On the other hand, the New Testament is filled with commands and instructions—many repeated from the Law—which determine right and wrong for us today.

So what should we do with the Law's commands? Are any relevant? How do we determine which are and which aren't?

Apologist Greg Koukl distinguishes the Mosaic Law from God's universal commands to believers today by comparing state laws to federal laws. State laws are limited to the state; federal laws are enforceable around the country. So a certain speed limit may apply only to one state, whereas laws against murder apply to all states. Koukl explains, "Universal moral obligations from the Mosaic Law are repeated in the New Testament. The things that no longer apply to us are not repeated in the New Testament. It's exactly like being in a separate state."[6]

So when statutes appear only in Israel's law, they properly apply only to Israel. When Levitical laws are directly or indirectly reiterated in the New Testament, they clearly apply to all believers. Murder, for example, is forbidden in Leviticus and throughout Scripture. Bestiality, prohibited in Leviticus, isn't mentioned in the New Testament but is prohibited indirectly: since the definition of marriage is clarified as between male and female humans, sex with animals is forbidden.

The New Testament includes three prohibitions against homosexuality (Rom. 1:26–27; 1 Cor. 6:9; 1 Tim. 1:10), which Jesus ratified when He confirmed the heterosexual definition of marriage (Matt. 19:4–6). The same can't be said of dietary and ceremonial rules and death sentences stipulated in Leviticus. So it's not hypocrisy to take the Bible as a whole unit, obeying the laws it repeats in both Testaments and placing limited laws in their proper context.

In fact, the new covenant under which we live provides even more comprehensive guidelines than the old, considering the laws of God are now written not only *to* us but *within* us. Jeremiah prophesied this (Jer. 31:33), and Jesus confirmed it when He noted that lust was condemned whether internally experienced or externally expressed (Matt. 5:27–28). We live under a different covenant ("agreement" or "contract"), not simply defined by prohibitions. Under grace there's no condemnation to those in Christ (Rom. 8:1), but also under grace holiness within and without are all the more expected of those same beneficiaries (Rom. 12:1–2).

SECOND RESPONSE: **Revisionists agree that Leviticus condemns adultery and incest. Isn't that hypocritical?**

Revisionists who support Argument 1 freely acknowledge that Leviticus condemns adultery, incest, and bestiality. If they don't acknowledge the commands against mixed fabric or eating shellfish—or homosexuality—doesn't that make them guilty of "picking and choosing" which verses they affirm?

THIRD RESPONSE: **Our position on homosexuality isn't founded exclusively on Leviticus.**

We do recognize Leviticus as one of five pillars of our position:

1. The Genesis description of the male-female union as an expression of God's image (1:27) and the answer to man's partnership needs (2:18)

2. Levitical prohibitions of homosexuality, among other sexual sins, repeated in the New Testament

3. Christ's confirmation in Matthew 19:4–6
4. New Testament condemnations of homosexuality, including Paul's term *arsenokoitēs* (ar-sen-ah-KOI-tays), derived from the Greek translation of these Levitical verses (see chap. 13)
5. The consistent witness of Scripture supporting the definition of marriage devised in Genesis and reaffirmed by Jesus

So while Old Testament law doesn't completely apply today, Leviticus still expresses and supports our position.

Heathenism: This refers only to homosexuality practiced as part of heathen rituals.

Employing what Gagnon calls "sophisticated attempts at undermining the Levitical prohibitions against homosexual behavior by spelling out an implicit motive clause that ceases to hold true in a modern context,"[7] some Revisionists claim these verses condemn only certain types of homosexuality, types no longer existing today, or condemned because of their exploitive, rather than their same-sex, nature. The "heathenism" argument concerns the first of three narrow categories of same-sex behavior we'll consider: *heathen, harmful, hierarchical.*

The Canaanites practiced homosexual prostitution in worship, and because Israel was commanded not to emulate them, some say these verses warn only against homosexuality practiced as part of heathen worship. So of course they don't apply to most homosexuals.

Revisionist Justin Lee, in his book *Torn*, writes about one of the Leviticus passages: "Some scholars . . . maintained that this passage was actually intended to condemn ritual cult prostitution, a form of idolatry in that culture that involved male-male sex."[8]

The Gay Christian Network quotes conservative pastor and author John MacArthur's Bible commentary to support this: "Judah's syncretistic worship was reflected in the practice of swearing by the Lord and, at the same time, by Milcom ... or Molech, the worship of whom included child sacrifice, astrology and temple prostitution."[9]

And conservative scholar Robert Gagnon, while clearly supporting the Traditional view, says, "I do not doubt that the circles out of which Leviticus 18:22 was produced had in view homosexual cult prostitution."[10] (Though this quote is sometimes misapplied to bolster Revisionist arguments, in the same paragraph Gagnon proves these verses apply to all forms of homosexuality.)

Since cultic homosexual prostitution thrived among nations surrounding Israel, Revisionists conclude that homosexual prostitution—not common homosexual behavior—is what Leviticus 18:22 and 20:13 address.

Both Boswell and Horner highlight the word "abomination" in support.[11] Boswell says the Hebrew *tō'ēvāh*, translated "abomination," refers to "sins which involve ethnic contamination or idolatry. . . . Often *tō'ēvāh* specifically means 'idol' and its connection with idolatry is patent even within the context of the passages regarding homosexual acts."[12]

Vines makes a similar but broader argument, stating that the word means something taboo to Israel at the time but not necessarily wrong today. For support he quotes Old Testament scholar Phyllis Bird, who said *tō'ēvāh* "is not an ethical term, but a term of boundary marking [with] a sense of taboo."[13] Vines lists behaviors to which the word applies that are not cultic, like charging interest on loans or eating pork, and writes: "So while *abomination* is a negative word, it doesn't necessarily correspond to Christian views of sin."[14]

In other words, the term *abomination* used in these verses allegedly means something ritualistically unclean (like sex combined with idolatry) or taboo only to Israel, but not something inherently immoral. So calling the average homosexual union an abomination misses the meaning of Leviticus, which forbids cultic sex between men, but not same-sex relations in general.

FIRST RESPONSE: **There are no contingencies in these chapters.**

Nothing in Leviticus qualifies these prohibitions. Nothing in their wording suggests that any of the six behaviors in Leviticus 18 and 20 are allowed in some situations, forbidden in others. One could argue that intercourse during menstruation is allowable today, but no contingency in Leviticus gives situational permission even for that act, much less acts of incest, adultery, idolatry, bestiality, or homosexuality.

Which leaves Canadian Old Testament scholar Gerald Sheppard, who supports same-sex marriage, unconvinced of this Revisionist position:

> I do not think that the texts in Leviticus can be read from a historical perspective as applicable only to cult prostitution because they stand in the context of other laws regulating general immoral conduct such as incestuous relationships, adultery, and bestiality. I find historical speculation concerning the restriction of the abomination formula to cultic violations weak and uncompelling.[15]

Fellow prohomosexual scholar William Loader agrees: "The wider context . . . goes beyond the cultic, as does the verse about bestiality which follows. Most [scholars] conclude that Leviticus 18:22 does condemn same-sex anal intercourse between males in general and is not restricted to particular settings."[16] And Gagnon drives the point home: "Moreover, the Levitical rejection of same-sex intercourse depends on Canaanite practices for its validity about as much as the rejection of incest, adultery, and bestiality."[17]

Which is to say, not at all.

SECOND RESPONSE: *Tōʿēvāh* (Hebrew for "abomination") **doesn't always refer to idolatrous practices and often refers to immoral actions.**

I noted in my 1996 book *A Strong Delusion* that one of the most well-known usages of *tōʿēvāh* has nothing to do with idolatry: "These six things the LORD hates, yes, seven are an abomination [*tōʿēvāh*] to Him: a proud look, a lying tongue, hands that shed innocent blood, a heart that devises wicked plans, feet that are swift in running to evil, a false witness who speaks lies, and one who sows discord among brethren" (Prov. 6:16–19).

Gagnon takes this further. Recognizing that *tōʿēvāh* in the Old Testament usually concerns idolatrous practices, sometimes as heinous as child sacrifice or necromancy (Deut. 18:9–12; 2 Kings 21:2, 6), he also cites verses in which the term applies to adultery (Ezek. 18:6), murder (Jer. 7:9), contempt for parents (Ezek. 22:7), lack of devotion to God (44:6–8), justifying the wicked (Prov. 17:15), oppressing the poor (Ezek. 16:47–52), or sacrificing a defective bull (Deut. 17:1), to name a few.[18] He summarizes, "Thus Boswell's contention that [*tōʿēvāh*] 'is used throughout the Old Testament to designate those Jewish sins which involve ethnic contamination or idolatry' is misleading."[19]

Boswell, Horner, and Bird inaccurately limit *tōʿēvāh* to cultic practices or boundary marking; its use is broader than that. And Vines is only partially correct in saying that the word "doesn't necessarily correspond to Christian views of sin." At times, it clearly does.

THIRD RESPONSE: The standard Old Testament term for male prostitutes isn't used here.

If homosexual prostitution is what God forbade in Leviticus 18:22 and 20:13, then at least one of the men in the verses would have been called a *qādēsh* (kah-DAYSH), Hebrew for "male prostitute." *Qādēsh* literally means men who were "hallowed" or "sacred" in the pagan sense, as in temple prostitution.[20] They're mentioned in Deuteronomy 23:17; 1 Kings 14:24; 15:12; 22:46; 2 Kings 23:7; and Job 36:14. (The female counterpart—*qedēshāh*—is mentioned in Gen. 38:21–22; Deut. 23:17; and Hos. 4:14.)

So the Old Testament repeatedly uses *qādēsh* when speaking of male prostitutes. Yet Leviticus 18:22 and 20:13 both use *zākār* (zah-KAR), meaning "male," referring to the men involved in the "lying together."

Revisionist James Neill calls this a reference to cultic prostitution: "While the term *zakar* can refer to a male, it is primarily used to refer to males with sacred associations, such as priests or men with special religious duties, or males dedicated to Yahweh in some sense."[21]

Neill is mistaken. *Zākār* appears eighty-one times in the Old Testament, first in reference to Adam, usually in reference to male humans or animals, and only twice—Deuteronomy 4:16 and Ezekiel 16:17—with any possible cultic connection. All other times it simply means "male." Which led Sean

McDowell, assistant professor of apologetics of Biola University, to consider the Leviticus heathenism argument and conclude, "When biblical writers want to prohibit cult prostitution, they do so clearly."[22] Author Don Bromley concurs: "It seems that if this specific practice [prostitution] is primarily in mind the author would have used this word [*qādēsh*], as done elsewhere, rather than a very general description of men sleeping with men."[23]

REVISIONIST ARGUMENT 3

Harmful: Leviticus refers only to harmful exploitation of youth through pederasty.

Revisionist Scroggs quotes the Jewish philosopher Philo, who said regarding these Levitical prohibitions, "Much graver than [marriages with barren women] is another evil, which has ramped its way into the cities, namely pederasty."[24] Scroggs comments, "Thus it is clear that when Philo reads the general laws in his Bible against male homosexuality he is thinking entirely about the cultural manifestation [of pederasty] in his own environment."[25]

Accordingly, adult men using boys or those of lower social status, like slaves, for sexual pleasure is the sin these verses condemn, not adult-to-adult homosexuality.

FIRST RESPONSE: **The Hebrew word commonly used for "boy" is not used in these verses.**

The most common Old Testament word for "boy" or "child" is *na'ar* (NA-ar), found 238 times. The second most common is *yeled* (YEL-ed), found eighty-nine times, then *vālād* (vahl-AHD), which appears twice.

But none of these is found here. Instead we find *zākār* and *'iysh* (EESH), both meaning "adult males." Had Moses meant to cite pederasty, then one of the sexual partners would have been called *na'ar, yeled,* or *vālād.* The original language condemns a same-sex union between two adults in plainest terms.

SECOND RESPONSE: **These chapters don't define sexual sin by age or status.**

Notice that incest-related verses in Leviticus 18 and 20 condemn all forms of intrafamily sex, age notwithstanding. Sex between siblings, in-laws, or parents and offspring have no "age of consent" clause. All are forbidden. (Note Paul's abhorrence of incest between adults in 1 Cor. 5:1–5.)

Now, of all sexual sins listed here, incest was the most likely to involve children. But it's forbidden without any reference to age. If incest is forbidden without regard to age, surely homosexuality, bestiality, and adultery also are.

As for exploitation by social supremacy, whether of a slave or a foreigner, the sexual treatment of slaves is covered in Leviticus 19:20–22 with no mention of homosexual exploitation. Foreigners were not to be mistreated (19:33–34), and 25:39–55 details slave ownership without instructions regarding sex. If God's prohibition against homosexuality only applied to relations between slaves and masters or Israelites with foreigners, these passages would address it.

But it doesn't, because male-to-male sex is forbidden across all lines, just as sex between family members is absolutely forbidden, a point Gagnon underscores: "There are no limitations placed on the prohibition as regards age, slave status, idolatrous context, or exchange of money. The only limitation is the sex of the participants. According to [Babylonian Talmud, *Sanhedrin*]

54a, the male with whom a man lays in Leviticus 18:22 and 20:13 may be 'an adult or minor,' meaning that the prohibition of male-male unions is not limited to pederasty."[26]

THIRD RESPONSE: **The damage is done, regardless.**

Sins of Leviticus 18 and 20, with the exception of intercourse during menstruation, violate the definition and sanctity of marriage conceived in Genesis and reiterated by Christ.

Adultery, incest, homosexuality, bestiality, and prostitution are thereby harmful in and of themselves, whether the treatment of one partner toward another is affectionate or abusive; regardless of age differences; regardless of social status. The damage of unions apart from marriage becomes its own mistreatment (see 1 Cor. 6:18). So the idea that any of these sins are condemned only because of their *context* is foreign to these chapters and the Bible as a whole.

REVISIONIST ARGUMENT 4

Hierarchical: This only condemns one man feminizing another.

Vines argues for rethinking Leviticus: "There are two main understandings of gender complementarity: hierarchy and anatomy."[27]

The "hierarchy" view is that men are superior, so homosexuality is wrong because it lowers a man from his superior position when he assumes a "female" role in same-sex intercourse. Vines says ancient writers believed this "male superiority" concept.

The "anatomical" view is that the sexes are inherently different, and therefore created in a complementary way that should not be perverted. This is commonly held by Traditionalists. But

Leviticus, Vines says, prohibits homosexuality for hierarchical reason, not anatomical. And if Leviticus forbids homosexuality based on belief in male superiority, then since we've discarded that belief, these verses no longer apply. For support Vines quotes ancient writers Philo, Plutarch, and Clement of Alexandria, all of whom condemned sex between men as something forcing one into a female role, "feminizing" and degrading him.[28] He concludes that these authors "don't talk about the design of male and female bodies—there is no mention of anatomical complementarity. Instead, they base their rejection of same-sex relations on a different belief: because women are inferior to men, it is degrading for a man to be treated like a woman."[29]

The anatomical argument rejects homosexuality because the Creator physically designed men to mate with women. But the hierarchical argument rejects it only because it lowers a man's status to that of a female—the view that Vines claims these verses express.

FIRST RESPONSE: **Philo's objections to homosexuality were not based only on hierarchy.**

Vines quotes Philo because Philo castigated male homosexuals for contributing to the "affliction of being treated like a woman."[30] But Philo also complained that the partner in the "male" role "renders cities desolate and uninhabited by destroying the means of procreation."[31] That's proof Philo disapproved of homosexuality also because it was nonprocreative.

SECOND RESPONSE: **Ancient writers from the same period as Plutarch and Clement of Alexandria condemned homosexuality without mentioning hierarchy.**

Vines also quotes objections by Plutarch and Clement of Alexandria based on the feminization of one man by another.

But ancient writers from Plutarch's and Clement's period (AD 46–215) condemned homosexuality with no mention of feminizing. They simply declared it wrong.

Aristides (AD 125) said, "Some polluted themselves by lying with males" and referred to "base practices in intercourse with males."[32] Athenagoras (AD 175) described "males with males committing shocking abominations."[33] Justin Martyr (AD 155),[34] Theophilus of Antioch (AD 168),[35] and Origen (AD 230)[36] all likewise condemned sodomy, while saying nothing about it denigrating one's manhood.

So while some ancient writers may have found homosexuality immoral because it "feminized" a man, some of the same writers, and many others, condemned it for broader reasons.

THIRD RESPONSE: **The argument places secondary objections over primary ones.**

When a behavior is forbidden for violating our Creator's intentions, there may be many secondary reasons for opposing it. But the violation of created intent remains the primary one.

For example, prostitution is forbidden because it violates God's intention for the sexual union, yanking it from the safety of covenant into the commercial. That's a primary reason for objecting to it. Secondary reasons may include the degradation of the prostitute, commonly at the hand of her "pimp." Or dangers of disease or violence to both parties, or public safety concerns. All of these are valid, but secondary.

A pro-prostitution apologist might successfully argue against these secondary reasons: Many prostitutes work independent of pimps, make good money, and enjoy comfortable lifestyles. He might even argue that biblical prohibitions against prostitution are only based on the writers' limited understanding of prostitutes, so prostitution can be legitimate. And if these secondary reasons were the only arguments against it, he might have a point.

But they're not, so the primary objection—the violation of God's intention for human sexuality—remains intact. Whether or not the act verifiably degrades the woman, whether or not it passes disease, whether or not it puts the public at risk, the primary objection is unmoved.

Likewise, homosexuality is forbidden primarily because it violates God's intention for the sexual union as monogamous, permanent, and heterosexual.

A prohomosexual apologist, ignoring the primary objection, could successfully argue against homosexuality's secondary concerns and show them to be insufficient: In many same-sex relationships both men are masculine, so neither is degraded. And since male-to-male sex needn't include anal intercourse, neither partner need assume a feminine role. He might even argue down biblical prohibitions based on "the writer's limited understanding." And if these secondary reasons were the only arguments against homosexuality, he might have a point.

But they're not, so the primary objection remains intact. Vines errs in assuming a cultural hierarchal attitude was the prime motive behind Levitical prohibitions when, in fact, it was not.

The Absence of Reference to Lesbianism

McDowell[37] and Gagnon[38] conclude we can't be certain why lesbianism is absent from Leviticus. McDowell offers Israel's patriarchal culture as a reason, while Gagnon proposes that only penetration was forbidden in these commands, which could occur in incest, homosexuality, adultery, or bestiality, but not lesbianism.

Ultimately, though, we can only guess. But since Paul describes lesbianism in Romans 1:26, its condemnation along with male homosexuality is unavoidable, whether spelled out in Leviticus or not.

The Final Argument

The most sweeping condemnation, though, lies in Leviticus 18:24–25, where God specifies His attitude toward the behaviors condemned throughout chapter 18: "Do not defile yourselves with any of these things; for by all these things the nations are defiled, which I am casting out before you. For the land is defiled; therefore I visit the punishment of its iniquity upon it, and the land vomits out its inhabitants." It was the acts themselves—not the way they were done, nor the ethnic group doing them, nor the masculinity or femininity of participants—that contributed to Canaan's national pollution, cultural destruction, and divine judgment. A sobering thought, considering God's later self-identification: "I am the LORD; I do not change" (Mal. 3:6).

Ten Talking Points about Leviticus

1. Homosexuality is "against nature" and "shameful" in Romans, excludes people from God's kingdom in 1 Corinthians, and is "contrary to sound doctrine" according to 1 Timothy. So criticisms of homosexual behavior hardly come from Leviticus alone.

2. We don't "pick and choose" which verses from Leviticus to take seriously. They've been picked and chosen for us by the New Testament's direct or indirect reiteration of still-valid Old Testament laws and its silence on those that pertain only to Israel under the old covenant.

3. The Traditionalist position is based on five points: the Genesis creation account, the Levitical prohibitions, Jesus's affirmation of the Genesis marriage definition, Paul's three condemnations of homosexuality, and Scripture's general witness to marriage as heterosexual, monogamous, and permanent.

4. Saying that Leviticus condemns homosexuality only when it's related to idol worship requires also believing that Leviticus condemns adultery, incest, and bestiality only when they're related to idol worship.

5. If Leviticus prohibits male prostitution rather than homosexuality, then *qādēsh* ("male prostitute") would be used, instead of *zākār* ("male").

6. If these verses prohibit adult-child sex rather than homosexuality, then *na'ar*, *yeled*, or *vālād* (the only words for "child" or "lad") would be used, instead of *zākār*.

7. Some ancient writers condemned homosexuality because it "feminized" one partner, but others condemned it for broader reasons. Leviticus condemns the thing itself, regardless of the partners' masculine or feminine roles.

8. The plainest arguments against homosexuality in these verses are anatomical, not contextual. It is the act itself, regardless of context, that is condemned.

9. We don't know why Leviticus never mentions lesbianism, but we know that male homosexuality is prohibited

here, and that Romans 1 condemns both male and female homosexuality.

10. Leviticus 18 lists homosexuality as one of many behaviors that polluted the land and brought destruction, no matter who practiced it, and no matter the context.

WHAT JESUS DID
OR DID NOT SAY

Never think that Jesus commanded a trifle, nor dare to trifle
with anything He has commanded.

—D. L. Moody

Christ's words either bolster or demolish our position. If He condemned homosexuality, the argument's settled. But if He was obscure, neutral, or approving of it, then the Traditional case unravels.

If He was obscure, we can only speculate what He thought,
and speculation's a weak argument. If He was neutral, then God
views the homo-hetero option as He did all but one tree in
Eden: No rules, choose what suits you. And if He approved of
it, then so must we.

Traditional Position

Jesus affirmed the heterosexual definition of marriage
by His firm reiteration of the Genesis definition, His

uncompromising endorsement of the whole Old Testament, and the absence of any word or action that condoned same-sex relations. In fact, His position was so clear to His hearers, His opponents, and His chroniclers that neither He nor any of them had any reason to bring up homosexuality.

But since none of the four Gospels records Jesus saying anything directly about same-sex relations, Revisionists see a void they try to fill by using *obscure, neutral*, or *approving* arguments.

REVISIONIST ARGUMENT 1

Obscurity: If He didn't condemn it, we can't know what He thought about it.

Two US presidents who identify as Christian have used obscurity to explain their support for same-sex marriage. Jimmy Carter said he felt Christ would approve, though he admitted, "I don't have any verse in Scripture."[1] Barack Obama cited the Golden Rule when announcing his evolved views, along with the Sermon on the Mount, which, he asserted, is "more central than an obscure passage in Romans."[2]

This would make sense if Jesus really was vague. Then for guidance we'd look to broader principles He taught, like love, justice, and mercy. But was He really unclear about this?

FIRST RESPONSE: **He reiterated created intent.**

It's true that within the Gospels, Jesus didn't mention homosexuality. But He plainly described God's intentions for marriage. In Matthew 19:4–6, when asked about divorce, He went back to the Genesis account of the first marriage, describing the original plan: "Have you not read that He who made them at the beginning 'made them male and female,' and said, 'For this reason a man shall leave his father and mother and be joined to his wife, and the two shall become one flesh'? So then, they are no longer two but one flesh. Therefore what God has joined together, let not man separate."

Here Jesus clarified the standard: Marriage is a male-female union, permanent, and monogamous. There is nothing obscure about this.

SECOND RESPONSE: **What falls short is sin.**

If Christ's standard is clear, then it's also clear that anything departing from His standard falls short of His will. Jesus said, regarding marriage, "This is what's right." He didn't need to also name all the ways to be wrong. He made Himself clear.

THIRD RESPONSE: **Jesus uncompromisingly endorsed the whole Old Testament, including the Leviticus prohibitions against homosexuality.**

During Jesus's earthly lifetime, until He sealed the new covenant through His death, the entire old covenant was still in effect. Nothing He said negated the old covenant, the validity of which He asserted in detail. For example, in Matthew 5:17–19, He left no mistaking His attitude toward the old covenant law: "One jot or one tittle will by no means pass from the law till all is fulfilled" in His death. The rest of the New Testament clarifies that the Leviticus prohibitions against homosexuality, which Jesus indirectly but definitely endorsed, remain in effect under the new covenant.

Everyone hearing Jesus—His followers, His opponents, His chroniclers—had reason to assume His endorsement of the Old

Testament. So He didn't need to clarify, nor did they need to ask, what He thought of homosexuality.

It's possible, in fact, that decorum prevented mentioning a homosexual act, though had Jesus encountered a homosexual caught in the act, we can assume He would respond with grace and truth similar to what He showed the woman caught in adultery in John 8.

It's also noteworthy that Jesus referred to Sodom five times, always emphasizing its wickedness (Matt. 10:15; 11:23–24; Mark 6:11; Luke 10:12; 17:29). He never specified the homosexual component of the city's evil, but He didn't need to. He knew the Old Testament Scriptures in detail, including the homosexuality emphasized in Genesis 19 (and underscored by other biblical references to Sodom—see chap. 9).

REVISIONIST ARGUMENT 2

Neutral: If He didn't condemn it, He didn't care about it.

This is the most popular Revisionist approach to Christ's alleged silence on homosexuality. Earlier pro-gay apologists like the Reverend Troy Perry[3] relied on it, current popular sources like the *Huffington Post* promote it,[4] and it can be found in pro-gay religious material online or in print.

Grammy Award–winning gospel artist Cynthia Clawson, for example, justifies her performing at prohomosexual churches: "We also know that Jesus never said anything about gay people. Not one word! How important could it have been to Him if He did not mention it?"[5]

In other words, silence means consent. No one's saying Jesus was ignorant of homosexuality, but some claim He had nothing to say about it, so He had nothing against it.

FIRST RESPONSE: **He may have condemned it.**

We can't know for sure whether or not Jesus mentioned homosexuality, since the Gospels didn't record everything He said. John said any written account of Christ is limited: "And there are also many other things that Jesus did, which if they were written one by one, I suppose that even the world itself could not contain the books that would be written" (John 21:25). Since no one knows everything He said, no one knows for sure that He did *not* condemn homosexuality.

SECOND RESPONSE: **He isn't recorded as condemning some other sexual sins.**

Jesus did not, in the Gospels, condemn bestiality or incest, though they are clearly condemned elsewhere in Scripture (Exod. 22:19; Lev. 18:6–18, 23; 20:15–16; Deut. 27:21; 1 Cor. 5:1). We don't ignore condemnations of these behaviors just because He didn't mention them. Nor should we ignore condemnations of homosexuality appearing elsewhere in Scripture (Lev. 18:22; 20:13; Rom. 1:26–27; 1 Cor. 6:9–10; 1 Tim. 1:10) just because He didn't mention it.

THIRD RESPONSE: **He didn't condone it.**

If Jesus approved of homosexuality, He had plenty of opportunities to say so. His mostly Jewish listeners believed it wrong, and He, God incarnate, knew that for centuries to come His followers would consider it sin. How easily He could have cleared it all up by saying: "You have heard it said you shall not lie with a man as with a woman, but I say unto you, that a loving relationship between two men or two women is acceptable." Yet He didn't. His silence lends more support to the antihomosexual argument than the prohomosexual one.

REVISIONIST ARGUMENT 3

Approving: He didn't condemn it—He condoned it.

Revisionists usually rely on Jesus's alleged silence for support. But some go further, saying He openly approved of homosexuality, citing as proof His encounter with a centurion and His references to eunuchs.

A. The Centurion and His Servant: Slave or Lover?

Matthew 8:5–13 and Luke 7:1–10 describe a centurion (a Roman captain of one hundred foot soldiers) pleading with Jesus to heal his servant, whom he loved deeply. Jesus agreed to visit the servant, but the centurion, confident in Christ's healing ability, said that wasn't necessary—if He only said the word, the servant would be healed. Jesus commended his faith and granted the request.

At face value the story seems clear: The centurion interceded for a beloved servant, whom Jesus healed. But some Revisionists see the centurion-servant relationship as sexual, based on the Greek word *pais* (PISE), meaning "boy" or "servant boy," used three times in Matthew and once in Luke. (Luke otherwise calls the servant *doulos* [DOO-loss], the common word for "servant" or "slave.") In writings outside Scripture, *pais* can also mean a lover who is subordinate, either a boy or a servant.

So argues author Jay Michaelson in the *Huffington Post*: "But *pais* does not mean 'servant.' It means 'lover.' In Thucydides, in Plutarch, in countless Greek sources, and according to leading Greek scholar Kenneth Dover, *pais* refers to the junior partner in a same-sex relationship."[6]

And since Jesus both healed the servant and commended the centurion's faith, the Revisionist argues that Jesus condoned their sexual love.

FIRST RESPONSE: **Nothing in the New Testament or in this story's context supports this meaning for *pais*.**

John Byron, professor of New Testament at Ashland Theological Seminary, points out that *pais* is a broad Greek term referring to many types of people. Its literal meaning, "servant" or "child," is interchangeable with *doulos*, also frequently translated "servant."[7] Outside of its four uses in the centurion accounts, *pais* appears twenty times in the New Testament—seven times describing a child or youth (Matt. 2:16; 17:18; 21:15; Luke 2:43; 9:42; John 4:51; Acts 20:12); three times describing servants (Matt. 14:2; Luke 12:45; 15:26); five times describing Jesus Himself (Matt. 12:18; Acts 3:13, 26; 4:27, 30); twice describing a young girl (Luke 8:51, 54); twice referring to King David (Luke 1:69; Acts 4:25); and once to Israel (Luke 1:54). It's impossible to believe that this word, otherwise used exclusively for children, servants, girls, Jesus, King David, and Israel—never with sexual implications—must be, or even usually is, a sexual term. In other literature *pais* does sometimes refer to a younger sex partner, but context determines whether the term is meant this way, and not a single use of *pais* in the New Testament has a context lending itself to a sexual meaning.

It's like the word *partner*, which can refer to a lover. *Partner* can also refer to a business associate, close friend, or workout companion. To interpret the word as sexual, the context has to be sexual, so insisting *partner* means "sex partner" disregards the other ways it's commonly used. Since the conversation between Jesus and the centurion provides no sexual clues, and because *pais* was used almost exclusively with no sexual meaning, there's no reason to presume the centurion and servant were lovers.

SECOND RESPONSE: **Love doesn't equal sex.**

The centurion's love for his *pais* doesn't imply sex. As Byron notes, a master's deep, nonsexual love for his slave is documented.[8] Common sense and experience also tell us bosses can have nonsexual love for employees (the existence of sexual affairs notwithstanding).

THIRD RESPONSE: **Jesus would not condone pedophilia.**

If the relationship was sexual, then it was almost certainly pedophilic or exploitive. So Jesus's condoning it would mean He condoned adult-child sex, or master-slave sexual coercion. Pro-gay apologist Tom Horner admits this,[9] as does the Revisionist site Would Jesus Discriminate?[10] and classical scholar Sir Kenneth Dover, who wrote, "The *pais* in a homosexual relationship was often a youth who had attained full height."[11] Jay Michaelson says of the centurion-*pais* union, "This is not exactly a marriage of equals. An *erastes-pais* relationship generally consisted of a somewhat older man, usually a soldier between the ages of 18 and 30, and a younger adolescent, usually between the ages of 13 and 18. Sometimes that adolescent was a slave, as seems to be the case here."[12] In fact, a sexual interpretation of this biblical story appears in the *Journal of Paedophilia* (a propedophile journal published in the Netherlands) alongside such articles as "The Life of a Christian Boy-Lover" and "Man-Boy Sexual Relationships in a Cross Cultural Perspective."[13]

No wonder Gagnon comments, "By the reasoning of those who put a pro-homosex spin on the story, we would have to conclude that Jesus had no problem with this particularly exploitative form of same-sex intercourse."[14]

Will anyone really accept such a conclusion?

FOURTH RESPONSE: **Healing is a gift, not a reward for virtue.**

Even if the centurion-servant relationship was sexual—a very remote possibility—nothing in the Gospels hints that Jesus's healing was a reward for virtue. He healed masses of people (Matt. 4:23–24; 8:16) without necessarily condoning the behavior of everyone He touched. Healing wasn't a stamp of approval but an act of grace.

FIFTH RESPONSE: **Commendation of faith is not commendation of behavior.**

Likewise, even if the centurion-*pais* relationship was sexual, the fact that Jesus commended the centurion's faith doesn't mean He commended the relationship. Rahab the prostitute was also justified by faith, a faith sparing her and her family from destruction (Josh. 2 and 6). But there's no indication that God commended harlotry just because He honored the faith of a harlot (Heb. 11:31). A person's faith is always a good thing. A person's behavior is another matter.

B. What Makes a Eunuch a Eunuch?

Jesus refered to eunuchs as celibate people in Matthew 19:11–12. Some of them, He said, are born eunuchs, some have been made eunuchs by others, and some choose to become eunuchs for the kingdom's sake.

Because the Old Testament Hebrew word translated "eunuch" is *sāriys* (sar-EES, from a root meaning "to castrate") and because the Greek New Testament term *eunouchos* (you-NOO-khos) means "castrated or impotent man," it's usually assumed a eunuch has been castrated, born without genitals, or otherwise sexually impaired.

Eunuchs are mentioned in both Testaments, sometimes as men having royal positions (Esther 1:10; Acts 8:27). Many were castrated to ensure they could guard a queen or harem without danger of sexual connection or plotting an overthrow, since they couldn't father a dynasty.

Because Jesus said some are born or choose to become eunuchs (castrate themselves or voluntarily become celibate), some say this broadens the term from one who's literally castrated or born without genitals to one who, for differing reasons, is sexually inactive with women.

Could homosexuality be one of those reasons? Horner,[15] along with many others, says yes. Recognizing that eunuchs were disqualified from the priesthood (Lev. 21:20) and limited in worship privileges (Deut. 23:1), he includes homosexuals among the outcast eunuchs, arguing that since they were born without desire for women, the term *eunuch* applies to them. This makes them recipients of Isaiah's promise that eunuchs would be given "an everlasting name" (Isa. 56:4–5), and it implies that Jesus described them as committed to the kingdom (Matt. 19:12).

In short, if *eunuchs* refers to homosexuals, then homosexuals can be seen as outcasts, of whom God approves, with a special place in His kingdom.

FIRST RESPONSE: **Parts of this argument are compatible with the Traditional view.**

Church father Clement of Alexandria wrote, "Some men by birth have a nature to turn away from women, and those who are subject to this natural constitution do well not to marry. These, they say, are the eunuchs by birth."[16] We agree that *eunuch* could refer to a male unaroused by women. But the term would apply to the sexually inactive, whether homosexual or heterosexual. We also agree that God welcomes and blesses the homosexual who, out of obedience, does not act upon his or her sexual desires.

SECOND RESPONSE: Traditionalists allow that *eunuch* might sometimes imply homosexual orientation.

Like *pais*, *eunuch* is a broad term, implying either no physical sexual ability, or no sexual arousal even if the ability is present, or possibly a homosexual orientation. We cannot be sure it refers to homosexuals, but we can agree that it might.

THIRD RESPONSE: Jesus's approval would extend only to celibates, not to homosexual behavior.

Yet even if *eunuch* is broadened to include homosexuals, Jesus here gave approval only to those who remain celibate. He would hardly limit the definition of marriage to one man, one woman in Matthew 19:4–6, then five verses later contradict that position to include homosexual unions.

Jesus said that obedience to His words was like building a house on a solid foundation, while disobedience was akin to building on sand (7:24–27). What He did or did not say, then, matters hugely, and to misread His words is to take eternal risks. To avoid those risks, we need only read His plain teaching, then apply it.

The Billy Graham Evangelistic Association agrees, answering prohomosexual interpretations of the Gospels:

> Sometimes it is said that the Bible does not record any words of Jesus about homosexuality, and therefore it must be acceptable to God. However, the Bible does not record sayings of Jesus about a number of other specific sins either. When people asked Jesus about marriage, He told them to remember what Genesis said about God's plan for marriage (Matthew 19:1–12). So, in this sense, Jesus did have something to say about homosexual partnerships. God only blessed sex within the committed marriage relationship of a man and a woman.[17]

Ten Talking Points about Jesus and Homosexuality

1. Jesus may not have mentioned homosexuality, but He defined marriage. He said what it is, thereby also clarifying what it's *not*.

2. Maybe Jesus did talk about homosexuality. John said that much Jesus did and said wasn't recorded, so how do we know?

3. Jesus didn't mention bestiality or incest either, yet all agree they're biblically forbidden.

4. Most of Jesus's Hebrew listeners believed homosexuality was sin. He often corrected misconceptions, so if gay's OK, why didn't He correct any "misconception" that it's not?

5. Jesus healed a centurion's beloved servant, but a man loving another man doesn't imply a sexual relationship.

6. The centurion called his servant *pais*, which in some literature means "lover." But no other New Testament uses of *pais* imply sexual relationships. The centurion story context implies nothing about sex, so it's unlikely *pais* means "lover" there.

7. *Pais* used sexually in other ancient writings doesn't just mean "lover" but also "boy" or "slave" in a sexual relationship. If Jesus condoned that, He condoned an exploitive adult-child or master-slave sex bond. Could anyone support that interpretation?

8. Healing isn't necessarily a sign of God's approval, just as sickness isn't necessarily a sign of God's judgment. Even if the centurion's relationship was sexual, Jesus's healing his servant doesn't prove He condoned the relationship.

9. Jesus praised the centurion's faith, not his relationship. Rahab the prostitute was justified by faith; Rahab's prostitution was never justified.

10. *Eunuch* could refer to homosexuals, though the word means "castrated" or "impaired." But Jesus defined eunuchs as celibate, whether homo- or heterosexual, and we agree that the abstinent homosexual is living within God's will.

PAUL AND ROMANS

The Bible is so simple you have to have someone else help you misunderstand it.

—Harmon Okinyo

A biblical position on homosexuality relies heavily on Paul's letters to Rome, Corinth, and Timothy, and though his statements on it are few, they're strong.

Vines calls Romans 1:24–27 "the most significant biblical passage in this debate."[1] President Barack Obama labeled it "obscure,"[2] but Revisionist Bennett Sims disagrees: "For most of us who seriously honor Scripture these verses still stand as the capital New Testament text that unequivocally prohibit homosexual behavior."[3] What Paul said *and meant* in Romans is hotly debated because it's so vital to the discussion.

He opens the topic with a broad statement: "The wrath of God is revealed from heaven against all ungodliness and unrighteousness of men, who suppress the truth in unrighteousness"

(1:18). The truths humanity ignores are available to everyone because they're shown through creation (1:20) and human conscience (1:32; 2:14–16), revelations dismissed by a God-rejecting race that's decaying inwardly, turning to other gods (1:21–23). The outcome?

> For this reason God gave them up to vile passions. For even their women exchanged the natural use for what is against nature. Likewise also the men, leaving the natural use of the woman, burned in their lust for one another, men with men committing what is shameful, and receiving in themselves the penalty of their error which was due. (1:26–27)

Paul then listed twenty-three other behaviors springing from our fallen nature (1:29–31), rebuked moralists who claim to be above such sins (2:1–16), and warned Hebrews who think having the Law and keeping it are the same (2:17–29). His intention was to prove sin is everyone's malady, so everyone needs the gospel.

Traditional Position

Paul called homosexuality a result of fallen nature, referring to the Genesis creation account to show how far humanity has descended from God's intentions. So far, in fact, that God's lordship over man has been replaced (1:21–23), God's design for man's sexual union has been perverted (1:26–27), and man's nature is hopelessly corrupt (1:28–32).

Homosexuality is not the main focus here, but it's prominently described as unnatural and shameful, clear evidence of the fall.

Polymorphous: Romans 1 doesn't describe true homosexuals.

John Boswell claims that the people of verses 26–27 were heterosexuals committing homosexual acts that were unnatural *to them*.[4] Their sin was having sex contrary to their true nature, as some heterosexuals today engage in same-sex acts when they're drunk, or in prison, or for experimentation—a *polymorphous* (many-forms) sexuality. The phrases "exchanged the natural use" (of the man) and "leaving the natural use of the woman" mean, according to Boswell, they left one orientation for another, abandoning their natural preference.

Accordingly, instead of an objective natural standard, "natural" becomes a subjective term, meaning "natural to you."

Scanzoni and Mollenkott hold this view,[5] also presented on the Gay Christian Survivors[6] and Religious Tolerance websites.[7] Vines likewise promotes it: "Just as those who are naturally heterosexual should not be with those of the same sex, so, too, those who have a natural orientation toward the same sex should not be with those of the opposite sex."[8]

FIRST RESPONSE: Heterosexuals don't "burn in their lust" for their same sex.

The men in verse 27 couldn't have been heterosexuals having homosexual sex, because they "burned in their lust" for each other. (Paul didn't say the same about women, but he described both male and female groups having the same experience.) A straight man might have sex with another man for release or experimentation, or even rape. But he's still not "turned on" to men. Paul described people hotly attracted to the same sex, burning for their own.

SECOND RESPONSE: **Paul's "exchanged" implies a willful choice of behavior, independent of feelings.**

When Paul said they "exchanged" the natural use of the opposite sex, he wasn't saying they switched their involuntary attractions from heterosexual to homosexual. The Greek word *metallassō* (meh-tahl-LAHS-soh) means "exchange, send away, cast off" and is the same word in verse 25: "[They] exchanged the truth of God for the lie." They actively rejected one, choosing another.

When you exchange truth for a lie, that doesn't mean you have changed objective truth. Rather, you've chosen to live in denial of it, rejecting it to believe a falsehood. The only change is your switch from reality-based thinking to fantasy.

Likewise, when you exchange natural behavior for unnatural, you haven't changed what God has determined to be objectively natural. You've chosen to reject natural behavior, embracing in its place unnatural behavior. Maybe unnatural behavior feels natural to you, and natural behavior *feels* unnatural. You may have no choice over what *feels* natural, but neither do you have the option of determining what is objectively natural or unnatural. These remain unchanged, and you choose (either with or contrary to your feelings) which behavior to embrace.

Someone who "exchanges" normal male-female relations doesn't choose to be same-sex attracted. But if he chooses behaviors that default to same-sex feelings, he has discarded normal relations for ones that *seem* normal to him. This could mean the individual was in a heterosexual relationship, then left it ("sent away, cast off") for homosexuality. Or it could mean he never was involved in a heterosexual union, but now rejects even the option of normal relating to embrace the abnormal. Either way, he has "exchanged" natural behavior for unnatural.

THIRD RESPONSE: **Sin coming "naturally" is no less sinful.**

If Paul meant the homosexuality described in Romans 1 was sinful only because it did not come naturally to these men and women, we should say the same of the malice, murder, envy, and other sins listed with homosexuality. We don't assume those behaviors are wrong only if they don't come "naturally." They're always wrong. Why, then, would we make homosexuality the only exception?

William Schoedel, a prohomosexual professor emeritus of classics and early Christianity at the University of Illinois, seems to wonder the same: "Paul's wholesale attack on Greco-Roman culture makes better sense if, like Josephus and Philo, he lumps all forms of same-sex eros together as a mark of Gentile decadence."[9] Lesbian scholar Bernadette Brooten, hardly an advocate for Traditional views, agrees: "I believe that Paul used the word 'exchanged' to indicate that people knew the natural sexual order of the universe and left it behind. . . . I see Paul as condemning all forms of homoeroticism as the unnatural acts of people who had turned away from God."[10]

So does Pastor Jeff Allen, senior editor at BarbWire, who concludes, "Every single person is born with an intrinsic inclination or tendency toward all types of temptations and transgressions, not as an inherited 'gift' from God, but as a spiritual consequence of the Fall of mankind (Gen. 3), which has significantly impaired and diminished our moral and ethical capacities."[11]

REVISIONIST ARGUMENT 2

Profuse: Romans 1 describes excessive lust,
not loving same-sex relationships.

Matthew Vines proposes that unbridled, out-of-control lust is what Paul condemned here: "Same-sex relations in the first century . . . were widely understood to be the product of excessive sexual desire in general."[12]

For support, he quotes a first-century speech by Greek orator and philosopher Dio Chrysostom: "The man whose appetite is insatiate in such things [sex with women] when he finds there is no scarcity, no resistance in this field, will have contempt for the easy conquest and scorn for a woman's love, as a thing too readily given . . . and will turn his assault against the male quarters . . . believing in them he will find a kind of pleasure difficult and hard to procure."[13]

Vines says homosexuality was frowned on by Paul because it indicated profuse sexual appetite that couldn't be satisfied just by women, so these men turned their attention to males. And since Greeks prized moderation and discipline, this out-of-control lust was unacceptable. But this doesn't describe modern homosexuals, so it couldn't apply to them.

FIRST RESPONSE: **None of Paul's language indicates excessive lust.**

Scenarios like Chrysostom's do happen, rarely but certainly. Some push the sexual bounds, "jumping ship" from opposite-sex to same-sex bedding, in search of something new.

But Paul describes behavior that's wrong in and of itself, no matter how profusely or moderately it's practiced. Let's review his exact terms:

1. "God also gave them up to *uncleanness*" (1:24, emphasis added, here and throughout this list). "Uncleanness" is from *akatharsia* (ah-kah-thar-SEE-ah), used nine times in the New Testament to refer to general impurity. The problem is the *impurity* of the homosexual act, not how excessively it's committed.

2. "To *dishonor* their bodies" (1:24), using *atimazō* (ah-tee-MAHD-zoh), meaning "disgrace" their bodies. The act itself is *disgraceful*, not just excessive.

3. "God gave them up to *vile* passions" (1:26), using the adjective *atimia* (ah-tee-MEE-ah), related to the verb *atimazō*. Using words from the same root twice, Paul said their *passions* were as *disgraceful* as the way they disgraced their bodies together, not just excessive.

4. "For even their *women*" (1:26) and "also the *men*" (1:27) use terms emphasizing biology (*thēlus*, THEY-loos = "woman"; *arsēn,* AR-sane = "man"). Both are used rarely in the New Testament—*arsēn* nine times and *thēlus* five times—noticeably when Jesus quoted Genesis: "[God] made them male and female" (Matt. 19:4; Mark 10:6); and when Paul stated, "There is neither male nor female . . . in Christ Jesus" (Gal. 3:28). Usually the New Testament word translated "men" is *anthrōpos* (AHN-throw-poss, used 559 times, generic for men or people in general), and the word translated "women" is *gunē* (goo-NAY, used 221 times). By using *thēlus* and *arsēn* instead of the much more common words, Paul was emphasizing the biology of the males and females committing homosexual acts. The problem is the *biological unnaturalness* of the act, not its excessiveness.

5. "Their women *exchanged* ['sent away, cast off'] the natural use. . . . Likewise also the men, *leaving* the natural use of the woman" (Rom. 1:26–27). The problem is the *discarding* of the normal act, not excess in anything.

6. "Men with men committing what is *shameful*" (*aschēmosunē,* ahs-khay-mah-SOO-nay, "naked" or "unseemly") (1:27). The problem is the *shamefulness* of the act, not its excessiveness.

Notice the emphasis on the impurity of same-sex coupling, and its classification as shameful based on its biological unnaturalness. The anatomical references to males, females, and "natural use" (*phusikē chrēsis*, phoo-see-KAY KHRAY-sees, "sexual intercourse as an occupation of the body") identify the physical unnaturalness of these actions as the reason for their moral and spiritual uncleanness.

Excess has nothing to do with this. Of all Paul's terms, only one comes close to meaning "excess": *ekkaiomai* (ek-KY-ah-my), "to burn strongly," used only here in the New Testament. All other terms in Romans 1:24–27 describe passions and behavior that are shameful, not because they're indulged to excess, but because they're indulged at all.

But couldn't *ekkaiomai*, the "strong burning" of verse 27, support Vines's point about excess? Doubtful. *Ekkaiomai* means only "strong burning," not "excessive behavior." When Paul wanted to describe "excessive lust" or "excessive sexual sin," he used the word *aselgeia*, found four times in his writings. Three of Paul's uses are translated "lasciviousness" in the King James (2 Cor. 12:21; Gal. 5:19; Eph. 4:19). *Aselgeia,* per the *NAS Greek Lexicon*, means "unbridled lust, excess, licentiousness"[14]— the exact sort that Vines says Paul condemned here.

Yet *aselgeia* isn't found in this passage. Had Paul meant to say the people of Romans 1 were guilty of excess, *aselgeia*, not *ekkaiomai*, is the term he'd likely have used.

SECOND RESPONSE: **Paul cannot be taken to mean that excessive heterosexual sex is "natural"; nor does he apply "unnatural" to excessiveness of homosexual sex, but to homosexuality itself.**

Verse 27 says these men exchanged the natural for the unnatural. Vines interprets this to mean they gorged on fornication with women, then, still unsatisfied, they turned to men. Using Paul's words, they exchanged their "natural" excessive fornication with women—what Vines calls the "easy conquest"[15]—for "unnatural" excessive fornication with men.

But can we possibly believe Paul thought excessively gorging on fornication with women was the "natural" use of women, which these men then exchanged? Hardly. And Paul didn't apply the term "unnatural" (*para phusin*, pah-RAH PHOO-seen, "against nature") to a man's (excessive) number of homosexual partners, but to homosexuality itself, whether a man had a thousand partners or one. Paul said the act, whether committed excessively or not, was unnatural.

REVISIONIST ARGUMENT 3

Pagan: Romans 1 applies to people who worshiped pagan gods.

Since Paul describes humanity as having known God, then rejecting Him for idols, some Revisionists argue that Romans 1 applies only to people who worshiped false gods. If so, then the homosexual behavior described occurred as part of pagan ceremony, so its connection to idolatry is what made it sin.

"The homosexual practices cited in Romans 1:24–27," Troy Perry states, "were believed to result from idolatry and are associated with some very serious offenses as noted in Romans 1. Taken in this larger context, it should be obvious that such acts are significantly different than loving, responsible lesbian and gay relationships seen today."[16] The Would Jesus Discriminate? website offers a similar take,[17] as do Justin Lee[18] and Jack Rogers, who explains, "The model of homosexual behavior Paul was addressing here is explicitly associated with idol worship (probably temple prostitution)."[19] Rogers goes on to paint a lurid description of sexual excesses featured in first-century Roman pagan rituals, including cross-dressing, self-castration, and orgies. This, he and others say, is what Paul opposes in Romans 1. Not adult-to-adult mutual relationships, but wild, ritualized orgies.

This sets up a division between "good" and "bad" homosexuality or, specifically, idolatrous versus nonidolatrous. Sex as part of worshiping idols is obviously bad, but has nothing to do with most homosexuals, who neither worship pagan gods nor participate in pagan rituals.

The argument, then, presumes Paul referred only to homosexuality among idolaters, not homosexuals in general.

FIRST RESPONSE: **Paul highlighted idolatry and homosexuality, not as related to each other, but as two prime contemporary examples of humanity's departure from God's design.**

Paul clearly divided humanity into those lacking God's law (Gentiles) and those possessing it (Jews). Both were guilty. In chapter 1 he named the sin of which all Gentiles were guilty: having a knowledge of God, through conscience or creation, then turning from it. Then he described two specific resulting sins: idol worship and homosexuality, both prominent at the time. Obviously, he wasn't saying all Gentiles were idol worshipers, any more than he was saying all Gentiles were homosexuals. But all were guilty of sins, whether it was one of these two striking kinds of offenses, or any of the offenses listed in verses 29–31.

Traditionalist author Thomas Schmidt recognizes this: "Paul . . . is suggesting that the general rebellion created the environment for the specific rebellion. A person need not bow before a golden calf to participate in the general human denial of God or to express that denial through specific behaviors."[20]

Romans 1 doesn't say homosexuality springs from idol worship or that the only type considered "unnatural" is the kind associated with it. Rather, Paul claimed all sin springs from man having turned from God. So the thread connecting Genesis 1–3; Matthew 19:4–6; and Romans 1 is undeniable, constituting what Gagnon calls the "echoes to the [Genesis] creation texts" in Paul's writing.[21] God ordained the male-female union, Jesus reiterated it, and Paul indicted its inversion as "unnatural."

SECOND RESPONSE: **Paul never qualifies homosexuality's condemnation.**

The argument imposes a contingency on these verses that doesn't exist. Search verses 24–27 to find one exception clause or a single word qualifying homosexuality as condemned only in one context but not another. You'll fail.

THIRD RESPONSE: **Scripture has no examples of "righteous" homosexuality, nor does it qualify any sin it condemns.**

Try searching the New and Old Testaments to find a positive example of homosexuality to balance out its several clear condemnations. Surely if Paul meant to condemn it only when connected to idolatry, we should find other examples of legitimate homosexual behavior. But again, nothing.

Now review chapters 1–3 in Romans and try locating one example of a sin mentioned in those chapters being portrayed as wrong in one context but allowable in another. Again, you'll fail.

Look at all other sexual behaviors condemned in Scripture—adultery, fornication, lust, lasciviousness, prostitution, incest.

Find one example of any such act called "sinful" in one context but "legitimate" in another. Yet again, you'll come up empty. It's not Scripture's pattern to impose contingencies on sexual behaviors it condemns. So how can we with any integrity impose such a contingency on homosexuality?

Gagnon confirms we can't: "The standard used by Paul for assessing homosexual behavior was not just how well or how badly it was done in his own cultural context but whether it conformed to God's will in creation for the male-female pairing."[22] And Don Bromley observes,

> The whole idea of human beings, as male and female, reflecting God's image is part of what is "self-evident" (or should be) to everyone. But according to the narrative of Romans 1, people stop recognizing the male-female created order, just as they stop recognizing the Creator. Paul isn't simply describing pagan idolatry, he is also describing the effects of an idolatrous mindset which doesn't recognize God's order.[23]

REVISIONIST ARGUMENT 4

Pederasty: Paul described sex between men and boys, not adult couples.

USA Today weighed in on theology and ethics when columnist Oliver Buzz, referring to Romans 1, wrote, "Paul most likely is referring to the Roman practice of pederasty, a form of pedophilia common in the ancient world. Successful older men often took boys into their homes as concubines, lovers or sexual slaves. Today, such sexual exploitation of minors is no longer tolerated."[24] Arland Hultgren of the Luther Seminary St. Paul seconds the idea,[25] which Scroggs posed decades earlier:

"Paul is only thinking about pederasty" in these verses. (Though Scroggs oddly admits in the next paragraph that the apostle's "opposition" to homosexuality is "not to be denied.")[26]

Relations between men and boys were common then, openly acknowledged among Greeks and well documented. This argument presumes that pedophilia, not adult homosexuality, was therefore Paul's subject.

FIRST RESPONSE: **Adult-child sex seldom includes the mutual lust of Romans 1.**

The men of Romans 1 experienced mutual lust, both parties burning with desire for each other (1:27). While it's possible for a boy to lust after an older man, such relations were and are usually marked by exploitation and inequality, the initiative and primary sexual pleasure being the adult's. Scroggs describes pederasty in Paul's time: "What must be emphasized is that the sexual encounter remained one of great inequality. The youth granted the older partner his body for sexual satisfaction without receiving similar physical pleasure, and perhaps by enduring pain or discomfort."[27] The mutual lust described in Romans 1 is a far cry from this.

SECOND RESPONSE: **Paul addressed lesbianism in these verses, which is almost never pederastic.**

This passage includes women (1:26), yet no one attempts to explain these lesbian relations as pederastic. Why, if Paul intended to condemn adult-child sex? And though adult-minor lesbian relations no doubt happened, virtually all descriptions of pederasty in ancient writings describe boys and men. If the prevalence of pederasty is what moved Paul to write this passage, then what moved him to also address lesbianism?

REVISIONIST ARGUMENT 5

Primitive: The Bible's authors didn't know what we know about sexuality.

Jack Rogers echoes countless Revisionists: "The Bible . . . has no concept like our present understanding of a person with a homosexual orientation. Indeed the concept of an ongoing sexual attraction to people of one's own sex did not exist until the late nineteenth century."[28]

The argument is twofold: First, orientation as a deeply ingrained response to the same sex was unknown or unrecognized in ancient times. Second, since biblical authors like Paul were limited in their understanding, they couldn't have known what they were writing about when condemning homosexuality. They saw it simply as a debased choice, not an inborn, unchosen characteristic.

FIRST RESPONSE: **Paul himself described internal attractions.**

Romans 1:27 states that men "burned in their lust for one another," a description of strong sexual attraction, not just behavior.

SECOND RESPONSE: **Sexual orientation (same-sex love and desire) was a known concept to ancient writers.**

In the *Symposium* (360 BC) Plato described women who "do not care for men, but have female attachments" and men who are "not naturally inclined to marry," along with male pairs who become "lost in an amazement of love and friendship and intimacy, and would not be out of the other's sight," who "pass their whole lives together" experiencing "intense yearning which each of them has towards the other."[29] Lesbian scholar Bernadette Brooten records ancient writings on lesbianism showing "both

Christian and non-Christian writers in the Roman world were aware of sexual love between women."[30] And Thomas Hubbard notes, "Homosexuality in this era (viz., of the early imperial age of Rome) may have ceased to be merely another practice of personal pleasure and began to be viewed as an *essential and central category of personal identity, exclusive of and antithetical to heterosexual orientation.*"[31]

Sexual orientation, then, was known of and written about in Paul's time.

THIRD RESPONSE: **Paul was well versed in ancient writings.**

Presuming a man of Paul's education to be ignorant of this seems a stretch, as Quency Wallace affirms: "It would be reasonable to assume that Paul, studying under one of the greatest rabbinical scholars of all time in the liberal Hillel school, would have received a wide range of exposure to Greek philosophy along with his traditional Hebrew training, to keep him abreast with the most recent philosophical knowledge of his day."[32] Indeed Paul quoted Greek philosophers (Acts 17:26–28, for example) and paraphrased up to eleven of Plato's sayings.[33]

FOURTH RESPONSE: **This argument negates the inspiration and authority of Scripture.**

No other sexual behaviors prohibited in the Bible—adultery, incest, bestiality, fornication, prostitution—are being legitimized simply because we know more about them today than ancient writers did. So even if we concede that we better understand sexuality than Paul or Moses, understanding the whys and wherefores of a behavior or orientation cannot legitimize either.

If all Scripture is, as Paul said, inspired of God (2 Tim. 3:16), are we then to assume God Himself had less knowledge about homosexuality than we have today? If we agree that God is the Author of Scripture, this Revisionist argument discounts not only Paul's awareness, but, more significantly, God's. Albert Mohler asks, "What else does the Bible not know about what it means to be human? If the Bible cannot be trusted to reveal the truth about us in every respect, how can we trust it to reveal our salvation?"[34]

Grasping at Straws?

Some revisions of Romans 1 seem like desperate attempts to avoid reading the chapter as it's written. Insisting on contextualizing verses 26–27 but taking the others at face value is reminiscent of W. C. Fields's alleged answer to why he was reading the Bible on his deathbed. "Just lookin' for a loophole," he quipped.

The same mentality seems to drive Revisionists' stretching and bending of Romans 1, a point Albert Mohler makes when critiquing Vines's work: "To get anywhere near to Vines's argument one has to sever Romans 1 from any natural reading of the text, from the flow of the Bible's message from Genesis 1 forward, from the basic structure of sexual complementarity, and from the church's faithful reading of the Bible for two millennia."[35]

Ten Talking Points about Romans

1. Romans 1 doesn't describe "excessive" homosexuality any more than it describes "excessive" fornication, "excessive" wickedness, or "excessive" murder. It condemns sins for what they are, not for how excessively they're committed.
2. Paul knew about same-sex passions and described sexual orientation in Romans 1:26–27, without needing the word *orientation* to do so.

3. Paul condemned homosexuality as unnatural regardless of its context—a loving relationship, an exploitive relationship, or a one-night stand.
4. The men in Romans 1 "burned in their lust one for another," meaning their relationships were mutual, as in adult-adult homosexuality, not exploitive, as in most adult-child sex.
5. The men "burned in their lust for one another," proving they were homosexual by orientation, not just heterosexual men committing homosexual acts.
6. Not one of the twenty-four sins in verses 26–31 is only sinful when it doesn't come "naturally" to a person. Homosexual behavior is no exception.
7. If the homosexuality of Romans 1 is immoral only if connected to idol worship, then none of the other listed sins is wrong, except when connected to idol worship.
8. Ancient writers recorded examples of homosexual love and passion, not just behavior, so Paul, a well-read man, would have been aware of these examples. He condemned homosexuality while understanding much of what we understand about it today.
9. Paul's wording emphasizing biology indicates he considered homosexuality's anatomical unnaturalness to be the basis for its moral wrongness. Patriarchy, orientation, and idolatry are irrelevant to his position.
10. The connections between Genesis 2; Matthew 19; and Romans 1 make it impossible to see Paul's criticism of homosexuality as "culturally biased." Rather, it is an inversion of God's original intent for all human sexuality.

13

PAUL AND *ARSENOKOITĒS*

The simplest explanation is always the most likely.

—Agatha Christie

Paul's three New Testament references to homosexuality are simple at face value, but in recent decades they've been portrayed as complicated passages requiring at least reevaluation, at most revision.

The Romans reference, covered in our last chapter, is a case in point, as is the subject of this chapter, the term *arsenokoitēs* (ar-sen-ah-KOI-tays). Just google it to see how controversial the word has become, and how central its definition to our subject.

It appears twice in Paul's letters, each time in a list of vices. The *New King James Version* reads,

- "Do you not know that the unrighteous will not inherit the kingdom of God? Do not be deceived. Neither fornicators, nor idolaters, nor adulterers, nor homosexuals, nor *sodomites*, nor thieves, nor covetous, nor drunkards, nor revilers, nor extortioners will inherit the kingdom of God" (1 Cor. 6:9–10, emphasis added).

- "The law is not made for a righteous person, but for the lawless and insubordinate, for the ungodly and for sinners, for the unholy and profane, for murderers of fathers and murderers of mothers, for manslayers, for fornicators, for *sodomites*, for kidnappers, for liars, for perjurers, and if there is any other thing that is contrary to sound doctrine" (1 Tim. 1:9–10, emphasis added).

In both passages, the word "sodomites" is from the Greek *arsenokoitēs*, which King James translates "abusers of themselves with mankind" in 1 Corinthians 6:9 and "them that defile themselves with mankind" in 1 Timothy 1:10.

Most translations agree the word means "male homosexuals." The *New International Version* reads "those who practice homosexuality" (1 Timothy) and combines the word with another to jointly mean "men who have sex with men"; the *New Living Translation* translates it "those [or 'people'] . . . who practice homosexuality"; it's "men who practice homosexuality" in the *English Standard Version*. The *New American Standard Bible* translates it "homosexuals," along with the *International Standard Version*, the *Jubilee Bible 2000*, and the *World English Bible*. The *NET Bible* has chosen "practicing homosexuals."

The *Darby Bible*, *Webster's Bible*, the *American Standard Version*, and the *English Revised Version* agree, in 1 Corinthians and usually in 1 Timothy preferring phrasing the same as or similar to the King James's "abusers of themselves with mankind," whereas the *Holman Christian Standard Bible* translates it, together with another word, "anyone practicing homosexuality."

The *Weymouth Bible* translates it as "any who are guilty of unnatural crime" in 1 Corinthians but as "sodomites" in 1 Timothy. The *New Oxford Annotated Bible* (2010) translates the word "sodomites," but takes a Revisionist interpretive stance in its notes, arguing that *arsenokoitēs* refers not to homosexuals but perhaps to prostitutes or "immoderate indulgence."

Strong's Concordance and *Thayer's Greek Lexicon* define *arsenokoitēs* as a male homosexual, as do the several authoritative lexicons listed by author Gary F. Zeolla: Walter Baur's *A Greek-English Lexicon of the New Testament*; Louw's and Nida's *Greek-English Lexicon*; Fritz Rienecker's *A Linguistic Key to the Greek New Testament*; Arthur L. Farstad's *The NKJV Greek-English Interlinear New Testament*; and the *Online Bible* lexicon.[1] Timothy Dailey of the Family Research Council concludes that no lexicon can be found that doesn't equate *arsenokoitēs* with homosexuality.[2]

The word isn't found in writings prior to Paul, so he seems to have originated it. It's a combination of two Greek terms: *arsēn* (AR-sayn), "male," emphasizing the sex of the boy or man (Matt. 19:4; Mark 10:6; Luke 2:23; Rom. 1:27 [twice]; Gal. 3:28; Rev. 12:5, 13), and *koitē* (KOI-tay), "couch" or "bed," with four New Testament uses, usually with a sexual connotation (Luke 11:7 is the exception, where the meaning is simply "bed"; Rom. 9:10 refers to Rebecca's conception; 13:13 discusses fornication; Heb. 13:4 refers to marital relations).

Arsenokoitēs, then, literally reads "male-bed" or "men-bed." Paul composed the term from the Septuagint, the Greek version of the Hebrew Old Testament translated two to three hundred years before Christ, frequently quoted in Paul's letters,[3] where *arsēn* and *koitē* are first found together describing male-male sex. Paul coined the term using the Septuagint's translation of prohibitions against homosexuality in Leviticus 18:22 and 20:13. In their English, Hebrew, and Greek forms they appear as follows:

Leviticus 18:22

English:	"You shall not lie with a male as with a woman."
Hebrew:	*"Et-zākār lō tishkav mishkevēy ishāh."*
	(with)(a man)(not)(you shall lie down)(beds)(a woman)
Greek:	*"Meta **arsenos** ou koimēthēsē **koitēn** gunaikos."*
	(with)(a man)(not)(you will sleep)(bed)(as a woman)

Leviticus 20:13

English:	"If a man lies with a male as he lies with a woman"
Hebrew:	*"Iysh asher yishkav et-zākār mishkevēy ishāh"*
	(a man)(who)(is lying down)(with)(a man)(beds)(a woman)
Greek:	*"Hos an koimēthē meta **arsenos** **koitēn** gunaikos"*
	(whoever)(sleeps)(with)(a man)(bed)(as a woman)

And While We're Talking Greek . . .

Another term Paul used relative to homosexuality is *malakos* (mah-lah-KOSS), found in 1 Corinthians 6:9 immediately before *arsenokoitēs*, and translated "effeminate" in the King James, *American Standard, English Revised, Webster's Bible,* and *Young's Literal Translation.* In some translations, like the *New International Version* ("men who have sex with men") and the *English Standard Version* ("men who practice homosexuality"), *malakos* and *arsenokoitēs* are lumped together to mean male homosexuals. Others, like the *Holman Christian Standard Bible* ("anyone practicing homosexuality") and the *Weymouth Bible Translation* ("any who are guilty of unnatural crime"), combine the terms to mean homosexuals of either gender, or even a broader category.

But the terms are distinctly different and should be read that way. The *malakoi* (plural) that Paul cited in 1 Corinthians 6 are more than just "homosexuals." That can refer to men assuming a female persona, or men taking a passive role in sex, or men dressing as women and prostituting themselves, or men who are soft and morally weak (see Matt. 11:8 and Luke 7:25, where Jesus is quoted using *malakos* to describe "gorgeously appareled" men, "clothed in soft garments," "who wear soft clothing," who "live in luxury").

In that sense *malakos* is much like our modern term *sissy*, a multipurpose word applied to cowards, weak men, effeminate men, men who dress as women, or (less often) to homosexual men—meaning always determined by context. And just as a sissy is not necessarily a homosexual, so a *malakos* is not necessarily an *arsenokoitēs*.

Paul might have listed both *arsenokoitēs* and *malakos* to condemn all forms of homosexuality, active or passive, in response to cultures where such behavior is viewed as less shameful for the man assuming the masculine role. Crompton views this as common thinking in Roman times: "For the Romans, homosexual relations were not in themselves good or bad. But to submit to penetration was to be feminized and humiliated."[4]

Consider prison life, where an inmate sexually exploits a weaker prisoner referred to as his "boy" or "bitch," who's thereby feminized while the exploiter retains "manly" status.

Paul says no to both. He indicts *arsenokoitai* (plural), suggesting the masculine role. And the term's derivation via the Septuagint from the Hebrew Leviticus phrase "lie with a male as with a woman" also indicts the other man's female role. And in 1 Corinthians 6:9–10 Paul also rejects the effeminate *malakos*, concluding (in conjunction with Romans 1) that *any* form of male-male or female-female sex is wrong, because it occurs between two biological "sames."

Traditional Position

These two passages condemn homosexuality, declaring *arsenokoitēs* unrighteous (1 Tim. 1:9–10) and, together with *malakos,* enough to exclude people from God's kingdom (1 Cor. 6:9–10).

Revisionist arguments about *arsenokoitēs* generally resort to either *reasonable doubt* ("it *could* mean something else") or *reinterpretation* ("it *does* mean something else").

One reason these arguments work is the disadvantage of laypeople when talk turns to Greek, ancient writings, and translations. We read an English word and its meaning seems self-evident, then an expert says, "No, I've studied the original Greek term extensively, and it means something else." Either we accept his word, or let Traditional scholars refute him, or we check it out ourselves, chasing Revisionists through an often-bewildering maze of evolving arguments and counterarguments. But that's unfamiliar, intimidating territory, playing with the big boys on their turf.

Yet in this age of online access and numerous credible apologists and theologians who've publicly faced off with Revisionists, the information to rebut their claims is available. And thankfully, you needn't be a scholar to use it.

REVISIONIST ARGUMENT 1
Reasonable doubt: It could mean something else.

To win a case, prosecutors must prove the defendant's guilt beyond "reasonable doubt." Even if the jury is somewhat convinced she's guilty, if the defense raises reasonable doubt, she'll walk. The Traditionalist bases his prosecution on biblical evidence against homosexuality. The Revisionist may try raising reasonable doubt, hoping his position will "walk."

Scholar Dale B. Martin, Woolsey Professor of Religious Studies at Yale University, both admits and defends a reasonable doubt position on *arsenokoitēs*: "I am not claiming to know what *arsenokoitēs* meant; I am claiming that no one knows what it meant [then]. I freely admit that it could have been taken as a reference to homosexual sex."[5]

Matthew Vines similarly acknowledges *malakoi* and *arsenokoitai* "could encompass forms of same-sex behavior,"[6] though he insists that, if they do, it's a different form than we see today. Gay Christian 101 cleverly points out that we cannot define a compound word just by its parts. *Mandate*, for example, does not mean "man on a date," nor does *butterfly* mean "flying butter." So how can we know the meaning of "male-bed" (*arsenokoitēs*)?[7] The Revisionist Ontario Consultants on Religious Tolerance claim, "Nobody knows for certain" what *arsenokoitēs* means,[8] as does Mel White: "Greek scholars don't know exactly what *arsenokoitai* means. And a good part of this tragic debate is that we don't know."[9]

Observing that *arsenokoitēs* is found only seventy-seven times in manuscripts from the first 2,100 years of Greek history, Gay Christian 101 lists fifty-six uses as references to rape, interspecies sex, prostitution, or pederasty.[10] The word's many conflicting possible meanings are thereby alleged to prevent us from knowing what Paul means by it.

Reasonable doubt, then, argues

1. Scholars don't really know what *arsenokoitēs* means.
2. Therefore *we* can't really know what it means.
3. Therefore we can't really know that it means "homosexual."
4. Therefore we can't really say homosexuality is *wrong*.

RESPONSE: **Context.**

How can the Gay Christians 101 scholars claim to determine which of their fifty-six passages use *arsenokoitēs* to refer to rape, which to interspecies sex, which to prostitution, and which to pederasty? Clearly, from the context of each use. Traditionalists apply the same criterion that these Revisionists admit using for narrowing or determining a word's meaning in a given passage. And Traditionalists use it to greater effect because they tend to strongly prefer each passage's most natural reading. Revisionists tend to ignore and violate contextually supported meanings.

When a word has various possible meanings, in a given context not all meanings are equally likely. In fact, most words in all languages are completely understandable in their contexts, and that's why people communicate successfully in every language. We know precisely what *weed* means in "I'll weed the garden" and "Don't smoke weed." We don't make a fifty-fifty guess what *weed* means every time we read or hear it. The same is true in Greek.

For example, in the immediate context of 1 Corinthians 6:9–10, Paul's pairing of *arsenokoitēs* with *malakos* provides a strong clue that *arsenokoitēs* means something unnatural related to gender. In the context of Paul's writings, he condemned any type of homosexuality in Romans 1, making "homosexuality" a probable candidate for Paul's meaning for *arsenokoitēs*. In the Biblewide context (and the context of all Greek writings) we see Paul as the likely inventor of the word, clearly based on the Greek translations of Leviticus 18:22 and 20:13, where homosexuality is prohibited.

We have other responses to the reasonable doubt argument, but since they also address the reinterpretation argument, we'll wait and let them speak to both, below.

REVISIONIST ARGUMENT 2

Reinterpretation: It does mean something else.

Reasonable doubt shrugs and says, "We don't know." Reinterpretation says we do know, we've gotten it wrong for years, and *arsenokoitēs* really means "prostitute," "pederast," or "pagan."

Prostitute

A significant challenge to our understanding of *arsenokoitēs* was the late Dr. John Boswell's 1980 *Christianity, Social Tolerance, and Homosexuality*.[11] For years it was the cornerstone of pro-gay theology, and though other Revisionist scholars now eclipse Boswell's prominence, his work is still influential.

Boswell determined that *arsenokoitēs* probably means "male prostitute" or possibly "immoral man," but not "homosexual."[12] Claiming the prefix *arseno-* (man) isn't the *object* of the word,[13] he said it therefore doesn't mean "men having sex *with* men" but instead means "men *who have* sex" or, more specifically, "male sexual agents." This, he said, refers to male prostitutes who service men or women, in keeping with Paul's several criticisms of prostitution. "*Arsenokoitai*," he wrote, "was the most explicit word available to Paul for a male prostitute."[14]

Pederast

Vines and Martin cite three post-Pauline documents: the *Sybylline Oracles*, the *Acts of John*, and *To Autolychus*—each using *arsenokoitēs*. They note it's not fully defined there but is listed among economic vices, having less to do with sex, more to do with greed or exploitation, like withholding wages or oppressing the poor. Sexual sins are condemned in other sections, but this one isn't listed in those sections. So, they conclude, since *arsenokoitēs* is listed among greed-based sins rather than sexual ones, it's not a reference to adult homosexuality. Rather, it's a sin of economic exploitation, probably pederasty (adult-to-teen sex), the economically disadvantaged youth exploited by the older, wealthier male.[15]

Pagan

Gay Christian 101 claims pagan worship was on Paul's mind when using *arsenokoitēs*, drawing support from conservatives like Dr. Leon Morris of the *Tyndale New Testament Commentary*, who wrote, "The inclusion of idolaters may point us to the immorality of much heathen worship of the day,"[16] and commentator Charles Eerdman, who said of Corinth, "The practice of impurity formed a feature of idolatrous worship."[17] John MacArthur's staff member Phil Johnson is also said to verify this view: "Most of the 'religion' in Corinth involved temple prostitution and debauched sexual behavior."[18]

(Gagnon challenges the notion of ubiquitous temple prostitution in Corinth as either exaggerated or false, noting "the scholarly consensus that there was no homosexual prostitution at the Corinthian temple of Aphrodite in Paul's day."[19] If

Gagnon is correct, the pagan argument is dismantled by that point alone.)

This, Revisionists say, proves that Paul objected, not to homosexuality, but to homosexuality practiced within idol worship, which has nothing to do with modern adult same-sex partnering.

First Response: Traditionalist translations are in the scholarly majority.

As of this writing (2016) the overwhelming majority of Greek lexicons translate *arsenokotēs* as a reference to male homosexuality, as do the majority of Bible translations. While majority opinion is not the final word on anything, it's significant nonetheless. This weakens both the reasonable doubt and reinterpretation arguments.

Second Response: The Septuagint links *arsenokotēs* with the Leviticus prohibitions of homosexuality.

The Septuagint was widely read among early Christians when Paul wrote to Corinth and Timothy. Bruce Metzger, professor of New Testament language at Princeton Theological Seminary, observes, "The fact that after the first century very, very few Christians had any knowledge of the Hebrew language meant that the Septuagint was not only the church's main source of the Old Testament but was, in fact, its only source."[20]

The early church's reliance on the Septuagint not only clarifies why Paul would coin a phrase from it but also clarifies the importance of viewing this phrase in an Old Testament context. Paul clearly derived *arsenokotēs* from the Septuagint's wording in Leviticus 18:22 and 20:13, a fact no Revisionist discounts. So if these commands condemn homosexuality, then *arsenokotēs*, coined from them, must condemn it as well. The entire case rests, essentially, on this point. (See chap. 10 for evidence of Leviticus's condemnation of homosexuality.)

This Septuagint link weakens both the reasonable doubt and reinterpretation arguments.

THIRD RESPONSE: **Greek language patterns confirm *arseno-* as the object of *arsenokoitēs*.**

Boswell's claim that the prefix *arseno-* isn't the object of *arsenokoitēs* is questionable. The late David F. Wright, author and professor of patristic and Reformation Christianity at New College, University of Edinburgh, showed that *koitē* in a compound like *arsenokoitēs* has the verbal force meaning "sleeping with." He illustrated: "Thus we have *doulokoitēs* (sleeping with slaves, not slaves sleeping with others), *mētrokoitēs* (not mother who sleeps around), and *polukoitēs* (sleeping with many others). Invariably—*koitēs* has, as one might expect, a verbal force on which is dependent the object or adverb specified in the first half of the word."[21]

Plainly put, if the word *doulokoitēs* (*douloi*, DOO-loy, "slaves," and *koitē*, "bed") means "sleeping with slaves," and *polukoitēs* (*polus*, PAH-loos, "many," and *koitē*) means "sleeping with many," then *arsenokoitēs* (*arsenes*, "males," and *koitē*) has to likewise mean "sleeping with males." And since Leviticus prohibits a man committing this act, it must refer to "males sleeping with males."

FOURTH RESPONSE: **Paul used another term to identify male prostitutes.**

Pornos (POR-noss) is the masculine of the Greek noun *pornē* (POR-nay), which is always used to refer to prostitutes in the New Testament.[22] *Pornē* means "female prostitute"; *pornos* most commonly means "male prostitute." It appears separately from *arsenokoitē* in both 1 Corinthians 6:9 and 1 Timothy 1:10, translated "fornicator" in most versions. But in fact it means "male prostitute" primarily, "immoral person" secondarily—somewhat the way we use the word *whore* for both prostitutes and loose persons. When Paul used *arsenokoitē,* then, he was clearly not referencing male prostitutes, since they would have been understood prominently included in *pornoi* (plural) elsewhere in both of these verses.

FIFTH RESPONSE: The pederasty limitation is unsupported even in Martin's cited sources.

Dale Martin's interpretation of *arsenokoitēs* as economic injustice, as with pederasty, reads far too much into the writings he quotes. None of his three sources, also cited by Vines, describes or defines *arsenokoitēs;* they simply call it something morally wrong, alongside other wrongs.

SIXTH RESPONSE: The idol worship limitation is unsupported by research or biblical context.

Interpreting *arsenokoitēs* as homosexuality practiced only in idol worship requires quite a leap as well. As noted earlier, Gagnon shows scholarly consensus doesn't support widespread temple prostitution.[23] Yet even if it was, nothing in the word compound—"males" and "bed"—hints at idolatry.

Additionally, 1 Corinthians 6:9 condemns both *arsenokoitēs* and idolatry, which makes little sense if the two were the same. But obviously they're not.

And as I've often pointed out, limiting homosexuality's sinfulness to one context requires similarly limiting the wrongness of the other sins Paul listed. But these sins are clearly wrong in all contexts. So is homosexuality.

So, Lightning Bug or Lightning?

Overwhelming evidence supports the Traditional under-standing of *arsenokoitēs*, an understanding challenged only through long, convoluted routes to vague and ultimately un-supportable conclusions.

Mark Twain once said, "The difference between the right word and almost the right word is the difference between lightning and a lightning bug." This is a case in point, the difference between "right" and "almost right" holding enormous consequence for church doctrine and conduct. To me, it seems the contention over *arsenokoitēs* is a classic case of overcomplicating a relatively simple term to throw doubt on its inconvenient meaning, at-tempting to open the door to its eventual redefinition.

Jason Velotta agrees, quoting Ross Taylor's observations on the *arsenokoitēs* debate: "The linguistic problem seems to me to be exactly analogous to this: suppose I have an Old Testament text which says, 'it is unlawful to lay bricks,' and I have a New Testament text that says 'bricklayers are lawbreakers.' It would seem inconceivable to me to say that Greek scholars don't know exactly what bricklayer means."[24]

Ten Talking Points about *Arsenokoitēs*

1. *Arsenokoitēs* is derived from the Septuagint's Greek transla-tion of the Hebrew Leviticus prohibitions of male homo-sexuality—a combination of *arsēn* ("male") and *koitē* ("couch" or "bed," usually with a sexual connotation).

2. Since the Septuagint was widely read at Paul's time, readers of his letters would easily understand this as a reference to homosexuality.

3. Nearly all Bible translations and lexicons translate the word to mean "male homosexual," not "prostitute," "idolater," or "pedophile." The meaning of *arsenokoitēs* has been clear for centuries.

4. If Paul meant the word to mean "male prostitutes," he'd more likely have used *pornos*, which, often translated "fornication," also references prostitution.

5. Paul couldn't have meant the word to refer to idolaters, because in 1 Corinthians 6:9 he names both "idolaters" and *arsenokoitēs* separately. If the two words meant the same thing, he would hardly have used them both.

6. The fact that some scholars are undecided on the meaning of *arsenokoitēs* doesn't mean all scholars are uncertain. There is, in fact, widespread agreement that it means what we've always thought it meant.

7. If *arsenokoitēs* refers only to homosexual prostitution, but not to average same-sex couples, then it stands to reason we'd find positive references to homosexual couples in the Bible, along with specific guidance for same-sex couples. But we find none.

8. If *arsenokoitēs* was meant to condemn homosexuality with a prostitute, could we assume other sexual behaviors in these verses—adultery and fornication, for example—are only condemned if practiced with a prostitute?

9. If *arsenokoitēs* was meant to condemn homosexuality as part of idol worship, could we assume other sexual behaviors in these verses—adultery and fornication, for example—are only condemned if practiced as part of idol worship?

10. Neither the word nor its meaning are obscure. Taken by itself or in context, it's hard to miss its meaning.

14

WHEN IT'S ALL SAID AND DONE

> How often I wanted to gather your children together, as a hen
> gathers her chicks under her wings, but you were not willing!
> —Jesus in Matthew 23:37

The high price of love is longing.

To love is to long for someone to be safe and happy. And if you're a serious believer, you know the person you love can't be safe or truly happy outside God's will.

You're basically at peace if the person is close to God; otherwise you live with a kind of pain, perhaps excruciating. It hurts when someone you love is in the wrong place, given over to the wrong behavior, or believing falsehoods. And from that place of hurt and concern, you speak.

You have to. You're an ambassador, and ambassadors express the heart and mind of their sender. You're also a human who sees and feels, and you're designed to communicate. Refusing to speak means turning your back on your task and your humanity, neither of which you can afford to ignore.

But speaking, while necessary, won't bring the final relief, because speaking of homosexuality isn't just a matter of "getting something off your chest." It's something you do in hope.

You hope what you've said will be heard, that the heart of the hearer will be softened, the mind enlightened, and that faith and zeal will rise in that person, causing him or her to say, as did Saul of Tarsus when truth confronted him, "Lord, what do You want me to do?" (Acts 9:6).

Sometimes your hope is fulfilled, and glory rains down. Truth is expressed, and received, prompting a sinner's conversion, or a believer's correction, or a prodigal's wake-up call to come home. And everyone parties.

It still happens. People are still responding to the gospel and coming to life, or responding to the Word and coming to truth. So homosexuals, whether unsaved, backslidden, or deceived, are still passionately loved by the God who relentlessly pursues them, long after we've exhausted all our efforts and arguments. So yes, hope can be realized.

But although truth is required, it's not all that's needed for results. God's sovereignty and human free will also come into play, two elements we can't control or predict. God's sovereignty determines how someone's life will play out, and free will determines the decisions she or he will make in the process. And when we love someone, we really are victims of both, because, putting it plainly, they jerk us around.

They wouldn't if we didn't care. If our hearts weren't invested, we could see someone dead in sin or deceived by it, and we could pronounce truth like an indifferent doctor pronouncing a diagnosis, then move on. Truth would be a lot easier, after all, if it wasn't accompanied by love.

But it is, binding our hearts hostage to another person's experience. Someone you love is wrong, so you speak truth, then wait for God's sovereign timing in the loved one's life, and for him or her to exercise free will to make the right choice. You ride a roller coaster up and down as a person comes close to choosing right, then backs off, then reconsiders, and so on. And while roller coasters are fun for those so inclined who ride voluntarily, you're strapped into this one against your will, and it can be a rough trip.

Terrific, too. It's exciting and even fun as we watch God use the truth we've spoken to further His purposes. Like the experience an elderly woman describes in the film *Parenthood*:

> You know, when I was nineteen, Grandpa took me on a roller coaster. Up, down, up, down. Oh, what a ride! I always wanted to go again. You know, it was just so interesting to me that a ride could make me so frightened, so scared, so sick, so excited, and so thrilled all together! Some didn't like it. They went on the merry-go-round. That just goes around. Nothing. I like the roller coaster. You get more out of it.[1]

When we say yes to stewarding truth, we board the roller coaster, consenting to the wild ride—the work of studying truth, the tension of speaking it, the joys from our friends' positive responses, and the griefs of their denials. All because we're bonded in love to those who may or may not join us in eternity . . . to those who choose intimate obedience or continue to rebel. Our hearts ride with them as they analyze, wrestle, rationalize, and hopefully, sooner or later, say yes to God. But we also risk accompanying them emotionally into the grief of no.

To my thinking, we who faithfully speak truth in love will ride with the loved one through the ups and downs of three stages—*confrontation*, *consideration*, and *conviction*—and with some to the joyous heights of a fourth: *conversion*.

Confrontation

Where God is working, there's confrontation. There has to be, because He's working in an environment largely hostile to Him and His ways. So said Jesus, and so said Paul, noting that this world is by nature in rebellion against God, filled with "the sons of disobedience." And, if that weren't enough, it's also governed by the original rebel, "the prince of the power of the air, the spirit who now works in the sons of disobedience" (Eph. 2:2).

Add to this hostile environment the sin nature we've all inherited, also at enmity with God:

- "The natural man does not receive the things of the Spirit of God, for they are foolishness to him" (1 Cor. 2:14).
- "There is none righteous, no, not one" (Rom. 3:10).
- "I know that in me (that is, in my flesh) nothing good dwells" (Rom. 7:18).

So here's a race of people naturally opposed to Him, living in an environment opposed to Him, ruled by a leader opposed to Him. Anyone speaking truth in such a place will of necessity be confronting error. Try taking that out of the stewardship equation, and you may as well close shop.

But this is nothing new. In fact, the legacy of the patriarchs, prophets, and apostles is a pattern of speaking truth which was at times received, frequently dismissed, sometimes opposed, and always confrontational.

Now, confrontation doesn't have to be intense or antagonistic; in fact, it usually isn't. When my wife tells me my shirt doesn't match my pants, she's confronting me. No big deal. Any time truth meets error, gently or loudly, that's confrontation.

And, you know, that's what this book has been preparing you for: confrontation. You are by now, I hope, better equipped to speak about homosexuality to someone either embracing it or condoning it. While your conversation will probably (hopefully) be polite and unremarkable, it'll be a confrontation nonetheless.

That's how it begins for all of us. The gospel confronts man's sinful state. Sermons confront our weekly need for upbuilding and guidance, and occasionally friends or leaders confront our behavior or attitude as needed. Since truth resides in a neighborhood of error, if redemption is to happen, confrontation between neighbors has to happen first.

Consideration

You speak, and the hearer mentally assesses what you've said, deciding on its accuracy or inaccuracy. If it's deemed inaccurate, then it's discarded. If it's deemed accurate by the mind, then it's transferred to the department of the heart, which, informed of the truth, must decide what to do with it.

A heart that's softened toward God receives the truth and conforms to it. But if it deems truth too inconvenient, too demanding, or premature, then the heart says, "Dismiss it," or "Oppose it," or "Decide later."

That's the consideration process: Truth is analyzed, rejected, opposed, filed for future reference, or embraced. Consider the way Festus analyzed and dismissed it: "Paul, you are beside yourself! Much learning is driving you mad!" (Acts 26:24).

Sometimes it's more than rejected. It's opposed, as when the Sanhedrin reacted so violently to Stephen's confrontation: "When they heard these things they were cut to the heart, and they gnashed at him with their teeth. . . . They cried out with a loud voice, stopped their ears, and ran at him with one accord; and they cast him out of the city and stoned him" (7:54–58).

Other times it's filed for future reference, as when Agrippa admitted his consideration of Paul's teachings without deciding one way or another: "You almost persuade me to become a Christian" (26:28).

And gloriously, sometimes it's embraced, no matter how ugly to admit, or how much it demands. An adulterous king embraced it after a faithful prophet confronted his rationalization for ignoring his sin (2 Sam. 12:1–15). So did a prodigal son when confrontation by memories of what he'd left behind brought him to his senses (Luke 15:11–32). Even a self-righteous Pharisee committed to persecuting Christians did, when confronted by Jesus Himself (Acts 9:3–6).

So the truth confronts, is considered, and leads to a decision. But I've left out one component that works in parallel with consideration.

Conviction

To convict (Greek *elengchō*, eh-LENG-khoh) means "to refute, bring to light, find fault, convince." John used it

- of the people gathered to stone the adulterous woman, after Jesus confronted their hypocrisy: "Those who heard it, being convicted [*elengchō*] by their conscience, went out one by one" (John 8:9).

- to quote Jesus regarding His Holy Spirit's word: "He will convict [*elengchō*] the world" (16:8). To this day we recognize conviction as one of the Spirit's primary works, by which the truth makes a person internally uncomfortable with sin and draws him or her away from it.
- to describe the light's (the truth's) exposure (*elengchō*) of men's deeds (3:20), leading to either hatred of the light or humble obedience to both truth and light.
- to quote Jesus: "As many as I love, I rebuke [*elengchō*] and chasten" (Rev. 3:19).

Also, in Ephesians 5:13 Paul wrote, "All things that are exposed [*elengchō*] are made manifest by the light, for whatever makes manifest is light."

Conviction, then, is what people experience when confronted by truth. We can't make it happen. We pray for it to happen, knowing full well that even if the truth we've presented gets past the committee of the mind ("Yes, I see that's true"), it still has the heart department to deal with. And the heart may, and often does, say, "I refuse this because of what it costs me." Only conviction can soften the heart; reasoning or arguing can't, because they address the mind, not the heart.

And this, I've come to believe, accounts for much of the unreasonable, extravagant, aggressive opposition we see today to the Traditional view on human sexuality. It is truth which confronts hearts, and people's hearts often love darkness more than light. The Holy Spirit's conviction makes them uncomfortable with what truth has exposed. So, not content merely to dismiss the facts, they hate them, and they stop their ears and rush in to annihilate the truth, like the Sanhedrin annihilating Stephen.

How else can we account for the levels of intolerance we see in defense of homosexuality—intolerance that people who simply disagree normally don't show? Generally, if Party A thinks Party B is wrong or even stupid, Party A simply ignores Party B. But not on this issue. Defenders of homosexuality sometimes seem, at least to me, rabidly obsessed with Traditionalists, fixated on their message, and consumed with a passion to destroy both it and the messengers.

It's as if people are saying, "I loathe what you believe, yet I'm afraid it may be true. But I despise that possibility—it makes me uncomfortable, which I hate—and I choose to silence my own consideration of your beliefs. But there you are, representing the truth by your very presence, let alone your words. Therefore I must hate and silence you as well."

And could it be that a number of additional influences— logic, nature, early teaching—all testify to truth, all aggravating the discomfort, requiring all the more energy to resist? I've often thought our culture's insistence on not just tolerating homosexuality, but legitimizing it with no room for dissent, is a massive exercise in counterintuition. The counterintuitive goes against our natural instincts—what used to be called common sense, but is not so common anymore. Now, sometimes that's good. For example, some proven scientific, archaeological, and theological truths have challenged what we intuitively believed. But sometimes forcing people to say yes to what's counterintuitive is wrong, and the vehement forcefulness of those defending the counterintuitive proves they themselves may not be fully convinced it's right.

It is my belief that we intuitively view male-female mating as normal and same-sex coupling as abnormal. I further believe we intuitively consider males and females distinct, not just anatomically, but also mentally and emotionally, and that attempting to truly change one's birth sex is impossible. Therefore, we also know, at some level, that a mother-father parenting team is the ideal standard. I believe that, intuitively and deeply, everyone believes all these things. Yet we are culturally committed to suppressing what we all intuitively accept as true.

So we indoctrinate kids, at earlier and earlier ages, to repress those intuitions by insisting they learn to accept homosexuality and transgenderism before algebra. We train five-year-olds not just to dismiss but to morally condemn their natural instincts about sex, so they will embrace a foundational worldview building block that is counterintuitive.

And anyone publicly expressing the intuitive view is subjected to what can only be called an overkill of shame. Careers end, businesses close, names are smeared in permanent ink, all because the victims said, "Something doesn't make sense here."

Conviction explains the gay movement's adamant discontent with mere legal victories. I believe the movement equates true victory with the eradication of the intuitive, the blocking of light, the once-and-forever silencing of everyone's reason and their own accusing conscience asking gently, persistently, "Is this really right?"

That's the power of conviction, fed by a combination of our biblical words, the hearer's conscience, and the Spirit's inner prodding. The spiritual explosion can kill or bring life, a decision largely in the hands of the exploder.

Conversion

When someone is converted from death to life in spiritual new birth, or from truth to error through repentance, the goal's been reached. Confrontation, consideration, and conviction lead to a big "yes." Someone is softened enough to enter into agreement with God, and strengthened enough in faith to believe He'll receive and restore the repentant. This we pray for and celebrate; complete conversion is our heart's desire for those we love.

Please realize, though, that some partial conversions are still good and substantial. The conversion of someone's perception of Christians or Christianity because of a believer's kind, intelligent words is good. The conversion of someone's attitude from hostility to warmth because of their positive interaction with an ambassador is good. And the conversion of a relationship from tension and misperception to healthy boundaries, mutual understanding, and mutual respect is good. We can treasure these important conversions, while still trusting for more complete ones.

The Honor of Truth Bearers

A steward is rewarded for faithfulness, not outcomes. We hope greater faithfulness means greater outcomes. But "other things"—such as God's and the hearer's will—come into play. And since those factors are out of our hands, we keep those hands on the plow, striving to improve our understanding, articulation, attitudes, and faithfulness to the standards we preach. Above all, we continue seeking deeper intimacy with the Master we serve.

Speaking of homosexuality is a small part of that life commission. Our more general commission is to speak of Jesus, His teachings, His invitation, His nature, and His soon coming. Any truth we can lovingly communicate to better prepare people for eternity, binding them to Him, is critical.

Therefore, if truth is vital to us, we will

- *Learn it*, knowing that we're created beings, that our Creator has placed truth within our reach, and that we are therefore responsible to know our Creator's message and what He requires.
- *Live it*, knowing that truth learned but not lived is of little use, and that hypocrisy was a sin that, like no other, got Jesus's dander up.
- *Express it*, because we know it is intrinsically valuable, that our hearers have capacity to receive it, and that its Author is able to work internally on the hearer's receptiveness.

And in learning, living, and expressing truth, we'll rejoice both in the privilege of stewarding it, no matter how it's received, and in the wonder of its fruit when it's embraced. This is the disciple's honor: participating as God's agents in the lives of the people He loves. This book is about that honor, and I'm honored to write it. I earnestly hope that it equips you, with both insight and techniques, to respond to one of the modern church's greatest challenges.

He who has My word, let him speak My word faithfully.

—Jeremiah 23:28

NOTES

Introduction

1. Laissez-faire capitalist (pseudonym), "Bill O'Reilly vs Bible Commentaries on Luke 6:37," *Free Republic*, December 20, 2013, freerepublic.com/focus/f-religion/3103779/posts.

2. "A&E Lifts Phil Robertson's 'Duck Dynasty' Suspension," *CBS News*, December 27, 2013, cbsnews.com/news/ae-lifts-phil-robertson-duck-dynasty-suspension.

3. Charlie Sheen on Twitpic, n.d., accessed December 24, 2015, twitpic.com/dphg5c.

4. Eliana Dockterman, "Boston Mayor Blocks Chick-fil-A Franchise from City over Homophobic Attitude," *Time*, July 23, 2012, newsfeed.time.com/2012/07/23/boston-mayor-blocks-chick-fil-a-franchise-from-city-over-homophobic-attitude.

5. Lucas Grindley, "Angry Alderman: Dan Cathy, You Can Forget about That Expansion," *Advocate*, September 23, 2012, advocate.com/business/2012/09/23/angry-alderman-again-threatens-stop-chick-fil-expanding-chicago-neighborhood.

6. Rahm Emanuel, as quoted in Ted Starnes, "Rahm: 'Chick-fil-A Values Are Not Chicago Values,'" *Fox News*, July 25, 2012, radio.foxnews.com/toddstarnes/top-stories/cities-move-to-ban-chick-fil-a-supporters-launch-day-of-support.html.

7. Ricardo Lopez and Tiffany Hsu, "San Francisco Is the Third City to Tell Chick-fil-A: Keep Out," *Los Angeles Times*, July 26, 2012, articles.latimes.com/2012/jul/26/business/la-fi-mo-san-franciso-mayor-to-chickfila-keep-out-20120726.

8. Including Davidson College in North Carolina (Tyler Kingkade, "Davidson College Suspends Chick-fil-A," *Huffington Post*, August 13, 2012, huffingtonpost.com/2012/08/13/chick-fil-a-davidson-college-suspends_n_1772685.html?utm_hp_ref=most popular); Johns Hopkins (Andrew Guernsey, "The Johns Hopkins Chick-fil-A Ban and the Coming Gay-Marriage Witch Hunt," *National Review*, April 22, 2015, nationalreview.com/article/417305/sandwiches-repression-andrew-guernsey); and the University of New Mexico (Timothy Dionisopoulos, "College to Hold Vote on Banning Chick-fil-A from Campus," *Campus Reform*, February 26, 2013, campusreform.org/?ID=4635), among others.

9. UTV (Ulster, Ireland) broadcast, original date unknown, posted as "Christian Nursery Nurse Fired for Saying Homosexuality Is a Sin—Lesbian Co-Worker Was Offended," YouTube, posted April 26, 2014, youtube.com/watch?v=TQrWRFlIGHA.

10. Laura Schlessinger, as quoted on Jonathan Lockwood Huie's Inspirational Quotes about Life, accessed December 11, 2015, quotes-inspirational.com/quote/you-liberal-anything-say-protected-129.

11. George Orwell, book review of Brigadier-General F. P. Crozier, "The Men I Killed," *The New Statesman and Nation* (August 28, 1937), 314.

Chapter 1 The Context of Our Conversation

1. Adelle M. Banks, "Study: Youth See Christians as Judgmental, Anti-Gay," *USA Today*, October 10, 2007, usatoday30.usatoday.com/news/religion/2007-10-10-christians-young_N.htm.

2. "Survey: Less Than 1-in-5 Give America's Places of Worship High Marks on Handling Issue of Homosexuality," Public Religion Research Institute, October 21, 2010, public religion.org/research/2010/10/less-than-1-in-5-give-americas-places-of-worship-high-marks-on-handling-issue-of-homosexuality/#.VmtUljjSnIU.

3. David Aikman, "Why Gays Hate Christians," *Charisma*, June 20, 2013, charisma mag.com/life/culture/910-christians-and-gays.

4. Jerry Falwell, as quoted in Daniel Kurtzman, "Jerry Falwell Quotes," About, accessed December 26, 2015, politicalhumor.about.com/od/stupidquotes/a/falwellquotes.htm.

5. Paraphrase of Benny Hinn's December 31, 1989, statement by unnamed web page author, "Benny Hinn," The Bible Page, accessed December 27, 2015, thebiblepage.org/avoid/hinn.shtml.

6. Hunter Walker, "Pat Robertson Claims Gays Deliberately Spread AIDS Using Sharp Jewelry," Talking Points Memo, August 27, 2013, talkingpointsmemo.com/livewire/video-pat-robertson-says-san-francisco-gays-deliberately-spread-aids-with-sharp-jewelry.

7. Michael Fitzgerald, "Donnie Swaggart Says Gay Rights Activists Want to Behead Christians—VIDEO," Towleroad, November 19, 2014, towleroad.com/2014/11/donnie-swaggart-says-gay-rights-avtivists-want-to-behead-christians-video.

8. See Ben Shapiro, "5 Big Wins for Militant Gay Pressure Groups," Breitbart, March 17, 2014, breitbart.com/big-government/2014/03/17/5-big-wins-for-militant-gay-pressure-groups.

9. Lars Grip, "No Free Speech in Preaching: Swedish Pastor Sentenced to Jail for Blasting Homosexuality," *Christianity Today*, August 1, 2004, christianitytoday.com/ct/2004/augustweb-only/8-9-12.0.html.

10. Ibid.

11. "Whatcott Defends Anti-Gay Flyers as Case Lands in Supreme Court," Tobi Cohen Postmedia News October 12, 2011, http://www.canada.com/life/Whatcott+defends+anti+flyers+case+lands+Supreme+Court/5540609/story.html.

12. Michael Gryboski, "Are Conservative Christians Being Censored by the Government and Social Media?" *Christian Post*, September 28, 2014, christianpost.com/news/are-conservative-christians-being-censored-by-the-government-and-social-media-127134.

13. Ibid. When invited to do interviews on Canadian television, I am more often than not given guidelines on what I may or may not say.

14. Mark Rice-Oxley, "Free Speech in Europe: Mixed Rules," *Christian Science Monitor*, February 8, 2006, csmonitor.com/2006/0208/p01s01-woeu.html.

Chapter 2 To Whom Am I Speaking?

1. Stephen D. Foster Jr., "Dan Savage Accused of Bullying Christians," Addicting Info, April 30, 2012, addictinginfo.org/2012/04/30/dan-savage-accused-of-bullying.
2. Larry Kramer, "Larry Kramer on the 20th Anniversary of ACT UP, the Government's Failure to Prevent the AIDS Crisis and the State of Gay Activism Today," Democracy Now!, March 29, 2007, democracynow.org/2007/3/29/larry_kramer_on_the_20th_anniversary.
3. "Survey: A Shifting Landscape: A Decade of Change in American Attitudes about Same-Sex Marriage and LGBT Issues," Public Religion Research Institute, February 26, 2014, publicreligion.org/research/2014/02/2014-lgbt-survey/#.VmteiDjSnIU.
4. Eugene, OR: Harvest House, 2015.

Chapter 4 Born Gay?

1. Simon LeVay, "A Difference in Hypothalamic Structure between Homosexual and Heterosexual Men," *Science* 253, no. 5023 (Aug. 30, 1991); J. M. Bailey and R. C. Pillard, "A Genetic Study of Male Sexual Orientation," *Archives of General Psychiatry* 48, no. 12 (December 1991): 1089–96; D. H. Hamer et al., "A Linkage between DNA Markers on the X Chromosome and Male Sexual Orientation," *Science* 261, issue 5119 (July 16, 1993): 321–27. Cited in Joe Dallas, "Born Gay? How Politics Skews the Scientific Debate," *Christianity Today*, June 22, 1992, 20.
2. Ibid.
3. David Ehrenstein, "Oblivion Couldn't Hold Bill Maher," *Los Angeles Times*, August 7, 2005, articles.latimes.com/2005/aug/07/books/bk-ehrenstein7.
4. "Answers to Your Questions: For a Better Understanding of Sexual Orientation and Homosexuality" (Washington, DC: American Psychological Association, 2008), 2, apa.org/topics/lgbt/orientation.pdf.
5. Michael Abrams, "The Real Story on Gay Genes: Homing in on the Science of Homosexuality—and Sexuality Itself," *Discover*, June 05, 2007, discovermagazine.com /2007/jun/born-gay.
6. Kathy Belge, "What Causes Homosexuality?" About, July 17, 2015, lesbianlife. about.com/od/comingoutadvice/a/Causes.htm.
7. Anne Fausto-Sterling, "Are We Born Gay?," *Psychology Today,* November 04, 2011, psychologytoday.com/blog/sexing-the-body/201111/are-we-born-gay.
8. William Byne and Bruce Parsons, "Human Sexual Orientation: The Biologic Theories Reappraised," *Archives of General Psychiatry* 50 (1993): 230–32.
9. Daryl J. Bem, "Exotic Becomes Erotic: A Developmental Theory of Sexual Orientation," *Psychological Review* 103, no. 2 (1996): 327.
10. Richard Pillard, as quoted in Dallas, "Born Gay?," 20.
11. Jeanie Lerche Davis, "Researchers Identify Alcoholism Gene," WebMD, May 26, 2004, webmd.com/mental-health/addiction/news/20040526/researchers-identify -alcoholism-gene.

12. Erin Cobain, "The Discovery of the 'Anger Gene': Could Anger Be a Hereditary Trait?," genomics class assignment for Davidson College, Davidson, NC, 2004, bio.david son.edu/Courses/genomics/2004/Cobain/angergene.html.

13. Denise Mann, "'Depression Gene' Linked to Response to Stress," WebMD, January 4, 2011, webmd.com/depression/news/20110104/depresssion-gene-linked-to -response-to-stress.

14. Richard A. Friedman, "Infidelity Lurks in Your Genes," *New York Times*, May 22, 2015, nytimes.com/2015/05/24/opinion/sunday/infidelity-lurks-in-your-genes .html?_r=0.

15. Ray Boltz, as quoted in Regis Nicoll, "God Made Me This Way," BreakPoint, September 6, 2011, breakpoint.org/features-columns/breakpoint-columns/entry/2/17901.

16. Stanton Peele and Richard DeGrandpre, "My Genes Made Me Do It," *Psychology Today*, July 1, 1995, last reviewed November 20, 2015, psychologytoday.com/articles/19 9507/my-genes-made-me-do-it.

Chapter 5 The "Change" Controversy

1. Alan Chambers, as quoted in Melissa Steffan, "Alan Chambers Apologizes to Gay Community, Exodus International to Shut Down," *Christianity Today*, June 21, 2013, christianitytoday.com/gleanings/2013/june/alan-chambers-apologizes-to-gay-com munity-exodus.html.

2. See Just the Facts Coalition, *Just the Facts about Sexual Orientation and Youth* (Washington, DC: American Psychological Association, 2008), apa.org/pi/lgbt/resources /just-the-facts.pdf. This edition of the booklet, though dated 2008, is still offered on the APA website as their current statement as of December 2015.

3. See Meredith Bennett-Smith, "More Than 30 Percent of Americans Think Gays Can Become Straight," *Huffington Post*, August 22, 2013, huffingtonpost.com/2013/08 /22/gays-become-straight_n_3790772.html.

4. Just the Facts Coalition, 3.

5. "Sexual Orientation," *Merriam-Webster Medical Dictionary* (Springfield, MA: Merriam-Webster, 2005), merriam-webster.com/medical/sexual%20orientation.

6. "Sexual Orientation and Gender Identity Definitions," Human Rights Campaign, accessed December 26, 2015, hrc.org/resources/entry/sexual-orientation-and-gender -identity-terminology-and-definitions.

7. "Practice Guidelines for LGB Clients," American Psychological Association, accessed December 26, 2015, apa.org/pi/lgbt/resources/guidelines.aspx?item=2.

8. Randall L. Sell, "How Do You Define 'Sexual Orientation'?" PBS *Frontline*, pbs .org/wgbh/pages/frontline/shows/assault/context/defining.html, as quoted in Glenn T. Stanton, "We Can't Protect Sexual Orientation Because It Doesn't Mean Anything," *The Federalist*, October 19, 2015, thefederalist.com/2015/10/19/we-cant-protect-sexual -orientation-because-it-doesnt-mean-anything.

9. Ann Tweedy, as quoted in Stanton, "We Can't Protect."

10. Sell, "How Do You Define 'Sexual Orientation'?"

11. "What Is Addiction?" American Psychiatric Association, accessed December 26, 2015, psychiatry.org/patients-families/addiction/what-is-addiction.

12. See "Understanding Alcohol Use Disorders and Their Treatment," American Psychological Association, accessed December 26, 2015, apa.org/helpcenter/alcohol -disorders.aspx.

13. Sobriety (800) 559-9503 (pseudonym), "Can Drug and Alcohol Addiction Be Cured?" posted on Addiction Recovery @ (800) 315-2391, March 23, 2008, addiction recovery.net/can-drug-and-alcohol-addiction-be-cured.

14. See "What Is Pedophilia?: Answers to Common Questions about Pedophiles and Pedophilia," WebMD, 2012, accessed December 26, 2015, webmd.com/mental -health/features/explaining-pedophilia.

15. "Stairway to Recovery," University of Pennsylvania Health System, 2003, accessed December 26, 2015, uphs.upenn.edu/addiction/berman/treatment.

16. See Rebecca Raphael contributor, "Exclusive: Anne Heche Interview," *ABC News,* accessed December 26, 2015, abcnews.go.com/2020/story?id=124031&page=1.

17. "Primary vs. Secondary Attraction," Asexual Science, August 12, 2013, asexual science.tumblr.com/post/69410727461/primary-vs-secondary-attraction.

18. See "Judge: Conversion Therapy Claims Are a Fraud," *CBS News*, February 11, 2015, cbsnews.com/news/judge-gay-conversion-therapy-claims-are-fraud.

19. See "Make Gay Reparative Therapy Illegal," Change.org, accessed December 28, 2015, change.org/p/barrack-obama-make-gay-reparative-therapy-illegal.

20. See Lila Shapiro, "This Bill Could End 'Gay Conversion Therapy' in the U.S.," *Huffington Post*, May 19, 2015, huffingtonpost.com/2015/05/19/conversion-therapy -ban_n_7322828.html.

21. See "Judge," *CBS News.*

22. See Shapiro, "This Bill."

23. "Therapies Focused on Attempts to Change Sexual Orientation" American Psychiatric Association, March 2000, 1, psychology.org.au/Assets/Files/reparative_therapy.pdf.

24. Ibid.

25. "The Damaging Practice of Conversion or Reparative Therapy," Faith in America, 2010, accessed December 28, 2015, faithinamerica.org/reparative-therapy.

26. Joseph Nicolosi, website introductory video, accessed December 10, 2015, joseph nicolosi.com.

27. Sigmund Freud, letter of April 9, 1935, as quoted in Colin Marshall, "Sigmund Freud Writes to Concerned Mother: 'Homosexuality Is Nothing to Be Ashamed Of' (1935)," Open Culture, September 26, 2014, openculture.com/2014/09/freud-letter -on-homosexuality.html.

28. Joe Dallas, as quoted in Susan Christian, "The Last Temptation: A Controversial Form of Counseling Promoted by Fundamentalist Christians, Called 'Reparative' Therapy, Has Led Some People to Reject a Gay Lifestyle and Try to Embrace Heterosexuality," *Los Angeles Times*, April 5, 1990, articles.latimes.com/1990-04-05/news/li-1108_1 _reparative-therapy/2.

Chapter 6 Same-Sex Marriage

1. "MCC and Marriage Equality," UFMCC, accessed December 28, 2015, mcchurch .org/overview/history-of-mcc/mcc-and-marriage-equality.

2. Judith S. Wallerstein, Julia M. Lewis, and Sandra Blakeslee, *The Unexpected Legacy of Divorce* (New York: Hyperion, 2000), xxviii.

3. The editors, "The Case for Marriage," *National Review*, September 7, 2010, http://www.nationalreview.com/article/245649/case-marriage-editors.

4. Abraham Lincoln, *The Complete Lincoln-Douglas Debates of 1858*, ed. Paul M. Angle (Chicago: University of Chicago Press, 1991), 128.

5. Hans Fiene, "Gay Marriage Isn't about Justice, It's about Selma Envy," *The Federalist*, March 31, 2015, thefederalist.com/2015/03/31/gay-marriage-isnt-about-justice-its-about-selma-envy/.

6. Marshall Kirk and Hunter Madsen, as quoted in R. Albert Mohler, "After the Ball—Why the Homosexual Movement Has Won," ChristianHeadlines.com, June 3, 2004, christianheadlines.com/columnists/al-mohler/after-the-ball-why-the-homosexual-movement-has-won-1266186.html.

7. "Lesbian and Gay Parenting," American Psychological Association, 2005, accessed January 2, 2016, apa.org/pi/lgbt/resources/parenting.aspx.

8. "The American Psychiatric Association Position Statement in Support of Legal Recognition of Same-Sex Civil Marriage," American Psychiatric Association, May 23, 2005, as quoted in a health policies review on Freedom to Marry, 2–5, freedomtomarry.org/pdfs/health_policies_review.pdf.

9. See Joe Dallas and Nancy Heche, *The Complete Christian Guide to Understanding Homosexuality* (Eugene, OR: Harvest House, 2008), 400.

10. Mark Regnerus, *New Families Structure Study* (Ann Arbor, MI: Interuniversity Consortium for Political and Social Research, November 28, 2012), doi.org/10.3886/ICPSR34392.v1.

11. Peter Wood, "The Campaign to Discredit Regnerus and the Assault on Peer Review," National Association of Scholars, June 19, 2013, nas.org/articles/the_campaign_to_discredit_regnerus_and_the_assault_on_peer_review.

12. Sotirios Sarantalos, "Children in Three Contexts: Family, Education, and Social Development," *Children Australia* 21, no. 3 (1996): 23, as quoted in Peter Sprigg and Timothy Dailey, *Getting It Straight: What the Research Says about Homosexuality* (Washington, DC: Family Research Council, 2004), 109–10.

13. See David Cramer in the *Journal of Counseling and Development*, as cited in Sprigg and Dailey, *Getting It Straight*, 96–97.

14. Sprigg and Dailey, *Getting It Straight*, 95–102.

15. Ronald Bayer, *Homosexuality and American Psychiatry: The Politics of Diagnosis* (New York: Basic Books, 1981), 3–4.

16. Ronald P. Rohner and Robert A. Veneziano, "The Importance of Father Love: History and Contemporary Evidence," *Review of General Psychology* 5, no. 4 (2001): 382–405, ritter.ist.psu.edu/misc/dirk-files/Papers/General/FatherLove.htm.

17. Anna Sarkadi et al., "Fathers' Involvement and Children's Developmental Outcomes: A Systematic Review of Longitudinal Studies," *Acta Paediatrica* 97.2 (February 2008): 153–58, republished as "Children Who Have an Active Father Figure Have Fewer Psychological and Behavioral Problems," *Science Daily*, February 15, 2008, sciencedaily.com/releases/2008/02/080212095450.htm.

18. Ibid.

19. Charles L. Baum, "The Long-Term Effects of Early and Recent Maternal Employment on a Child's Academic Achievement," *Journal of Family Issues* 25, no. 1 (2004): 29–60, DOI: 10.1177/0192513X03255461, jfi.sagepub.com/cgi/content/abstract/25/1/29.

20. David Popenoe, *Life without Father: Compelling New Evidence That Fatherhood and Marriage Are Indispensable for the Good of Children and Society* (New York: Free Press, 1996), 197, as quoted in Jenny Tyree, "Mom and Dad: Kids Need Both," Citizen Link, June 15, 2010, https://www.focusonthefamily.com/socialissues/marriage/teach -your-children-about-marriage/mom-and-dad-children-need-both.

21. Kristin Anderson Moore, Susan M. Jekielek, and Carol Emig, "Marriage from a Child's Perspective: How Does Family Structure Affect Children, and What Can We Do about It?" Child Trends, June 2002, 1, childtrends.org/wp-content/uploads/2013 /03/MarriageRB602.pdf.

22. Randi James, "Stepmothers Cannot Replace Biological Mothers," April 28, 2010, posted by Claudine Dombrowski on her blog *Battered Mothers: A Human Rights Issue*, angelzfury.wordpress.com/2010/08/28/pa-hrefhttpwwwrandijamescom200905step motherscannotreplacebiologicalhtmlby-awesome-randi-jamesappstrongstepmothers -replace-biological-mothers-emphasis-minestrongppstrongmythstrong-stepmothers -acceptabl.

23. Mary Park, "Are Married Parents Really Better for Children?" Center for Law and Social Policy, May 2003, 1, clasp.org/resources-and-publications/states/0086.pdf.

24. David Blankenhorn, "Protecting Marriage to Protect Children," *Los Angeles Times*, September 16, 2008, http://www.latimes.com/la-oe-blankenhorn19-2008sep 19-story.html.

25. Ibid.

26. Clint Eastwood, Jay-Z, Janet Jackson, all as quoted in "66 Inspirational Quotes about Gay Marriage," *Huffington Post*, March 23, 2013, huffingtonpost.com/2013/03 /25/gay-marriage-quotes_n_2947825.html.

27. Andrew Sullivan, *Virtually Normal* (New York: Vintage, 1996), 202–3.

28. Michelangelo Signorile, "Bridal Wave," *OUT*, December/January 1994–1995, 161.

29. Paula Ettelbrick, "Since When Is Marriage a Path to Liberation?," in *Lesbians, Gay Men and the Law*, ed. William Rubenstein (New York: New Press, 1993), 401–5.

30. "The New Monogamy," *New York,* November 21, 2005, nymag.com/lifestyle/sex /annual/2005/15063/index2.html.

31. Ibid.

32. Scott Jamesjan, "Most Successful Gay Marriages Share an Open Secret," *New York Times*, January 28, 2010, nytimes.com/2010/01/29/us/29sfmetro.html?_r=0.

33. Ibid.

34. Steven W. Thrasher, "Master Bedroom, Extra Closet: The Truth about Gay Marriage," Gawker, June 19, 2013, gawker.com/master-bedroom-extra-closet-the-truth-about -gay-marri-514348538.

35. Hanna Rosin, "The Dirty Little Secret: Most Gay Couples Aren't Monogamous," The XX Factor, June 26, 2013, slate.com/blogs/xx_factor/2013/06/26/most_gay_couples _aren_t_monogamous_will_straight_couples_go_monogamish.html.

36. Whoopi Goldberg, "Whoopi Fights Back," YouTube, uploaded October 25, 2010, http://youtu.be/_5qQmKsujJg.

37. Barack Obama, as quoted in Fred Lucas, "Obama: Gay Marriage Ruling Is a 'Victory for America,'" *The Blaze*, June 26, 2015, theblaze.com/stories/2015/06/26 /obama-gay-marriage-ruling-is-a-victory-for-america.

38. Joel Gehrke, "Obama's Lawyer: Religious Institutions May Lose Tax-Exempt Status If Court Rules for Gay Marriage," *National Review*, April 28, 2015, national

review.com/article/417597/obamas-lawyer-religious-institutions-may-lose-tax-exempt
-status-if-court-rules-gay.

39. Gregory Cochran, "Why Marriage Must Remain Traditional," Gregory C.
Cochran, May 17, 2012, gregoryccochran.com/2012/05/17/dont-mess-with-marriage
/#comment-11628.

Chapter 7 Homophobia, Hate, Hypocrisy, and Harm

1. Richard Isay, *Being Homosexual* (New York: Farrar, Straus, and Giroux, 1989), 145.

2. "Diseases and Conditions: Phobias," Mayo Clinic, February 8, 2014, mayoclinic
.org/diseases-conditions/phobias/basics/symptoms/con-20023478.

3. Sullivan, *Virtually Normal*, 212.

4. *Merriam-Webster Online*, s.v. "hatred," accessed December 28, 2015, merriam
-webster.com/dictionary/hatred.

5. Brian McLaren, as quoted in Tony Jones, "Brian McLaren's View on Homosexuality," *Theoblogy*, October 8, 2012, patheos.com/blogs/tonyjones/2012/10/08/brian
-mclaren-clarifies-his-view-on-homosexuality.

6. David Gushee, as quoted in Aaron D. Weaver, "David Gushee & Path to Discern-
ment on Homosexuality," *The Big Daddy Weave*, July 26, 2008, thebigdaddyweave.com
/2008/07/david-gushee-path-to-discernment-on-homosexuality.html.

7. Tim Stafford, "The Abolitionists," *Christianity Today*, January 1, 1992, ctlibrary
.com/ch/1992/issue33/3321.html.

8. George E. Curry, "Jerry Falwell's Racist Past," George E. Curry, May 21, 2007,
http://198.154.238.87/index.php/contact/archives/185-chronicle-archives/2471.

9. W. A. Criswell, as quoted in Curtis W. Freeman, "'Never Had I Been So Blind':
W. A. Criswell's 'Change' on Racial Segregation," *Journal of Southern Religion* 10 (2007):
1, jsr.fsu.edu/Volume10/Freeman.pdf.

10. Nina Mandell, "Dan Savage Accused of Bullying after Journalism Conference,"
New York Daily News, May 2, 2012, nydailynews.com/news/national/dan-savage-accused
-bullying-journalism-conference-article-1.1071153.

11. Robert Gagnon, "Slavery, Homosexuality, and the Bible: A Response," RobGagnon
.net, 2004, accessed December 28, 2014, robgagnon.net/RespKrehbiel.htm.

12. Joe Dallas, "When Soulforce Calls," *Christian Research Journal* 32, no. 2 (2009),
equip.org/article/when-soulforce-calls.

13. Daryl Cornett, "LGBT and the Church: An Interaction with David Gushee,"
A Pastor's Progress, January 7, 2015, darylcornett.blogspot.co.nz/2015/01/lgbt-church
-interaction-with-david.html.

14. Paul Walker's decision, posted in Good As You (pseudonym), "California Prop
8 Ruling (August 2010)," SCRIBD, accessed December 28, 2015, scribd.com/doc/353
74462/California-Prop-8-Ruling-August-2010.

15. Mel White, "Religion Gone Bad," Robert Shepherd website, accessed December
28, 2015, geocities.ws/cott1388/matson-mowder.html.

16. Reed Irvine and Cliff Kincaid, "Hate Campaign over Hate Crimes," Media Monitor, November 2, 1998, aim.org/publications/media_monitor/1998/11/02.htm.

17. Transcripted interview with Kathy Griffin, Wanda Sykes, and Lance Bass from
October 4, 2010, broadcast of *Larry King Live!* Cable News Network, transcripts.cnn
.com/TRANSCRIPTS/1010/04/lkl.01.html.

Chapter 8 Gay Christians

1. See "History of MCC," Metropolitan Community Church, Fall 2004, mccchurch.org/overview/history-of-mcc.
2. See "What Is Dignity?," Dignity, accessed December 28, 2015, dignityusa.org/article/what-dignity.
3. See "Dr. Ralph Blair—Founder of EC," Evangelicals Concerned, accessed December 28, 2015, ecinc.org/dr-ralph-blair-founder-of-ec.
4. John Boswell, *Christianity, Social Tolerance, and Homosexuality: Gay People in Western Europe from the Beginning of the Christian Era to the Fourteenth Century* (Chicago: University of Chicago Press, 1980).
5. Letha Scanzoni and Virginia Mollenkott, *Is the Homosexual My Neighbor?* (New York: Harper and Row, 1978).
6. See ELCA, "Stances of Faiths on LGBT Issues: Evangelical Lutheran Church in America," Human Rights Campaign, April 27, 2015, hrc.org/resources/stances-of-faiths-on-lgbt-issues-evangelical-lutheran-church-in-america.
7. See "LGBT in the Church," Episcopal Church, accessed December 28, 2015, episcopalchurch.org/page/lgbt-church.
8. See "Stances of Faiths on LGBT Issues: Presbyterian Church (USA)," Human Rights Campaign, March 18, 2015, hrc.org/resources/stances-of-faiths-on-lgbt-issues-presbyterian-church-usa.
9. Ray Nothstine, "Tony Campolo Finally Capitulates on Gay Marriage; Cites Wife and Gay Friends as Influences for Changing Position," *Christian Post*, June 9, 2015, christianpost.com/news/tony-campolo-finally-capitulates-on-gay-marriage-cites-wife-and-gay-friends-as-influences-for-changing-position-140133/#ZOuAc6McvmCU09mB.99.
10. Jonathan Merritt, "Leading Evangelical Ethicist David Gushee Is Now Pro-LGBT," Religion News Service, October 24, 2014, jonathanmerritt.religionnews.com/2014/10/24/david-gushee-lgbt-homosexuality-matter.
11. Nicola Menzie, "Rob Bell on Gay Marriage Support: God Pulling Us Ahead to Affirm Gay Brothers, Sisters," *Christian Post*, March 22, 2013, christianpost.com/news/rob-bell-on-gay-marriage-support-god-pulling-us-ahead-to-affirm-gay-brothers-sisters-92395/#HKL4OZshVIUimdb6.99.
12. Jonathan Merritt, "Is the Christian Music Industry Liberalizing on Gay Marriage?," *The Week*, August 21, 2014, theweek.com/articles/444405/christian-music-industry-liberalizing-gay-marriage.
13. "Ray Boltz Comes Out," *Christianity Today,* September 12, 2008, christianitytoday.com/gleanings/2008/september/ray-boltz-comes-out.html.
14. Billy Hallowell, "Gay Singer Jennifer Knapp Details Her Sexuality," The Blaze, September 4, 2012, theblaze.com/stories/2012/09/04/gay-ex-christian-singer-jennifer-knapp-details-her-sexuality-why-she-tried-to-undo-her-religion.
15. Merritt, "Christian Music Industry."
16. Tony Perkins, "Christian Band Drums Up Support for Gay Marriage," *Charisma News*, April 29, 2014, charismanews.com/opinion/43652-christian-band-drums-up-support-for-gay-marriage.
17. Merritt, "Christian Music Industry."

18. Rachel Held Evans, "Unstoppable Grace: Thoughts on the Gay Christian Network Conference," *Rachel Held Evans* blog, January 15, 2014, rachelheldevans.com/blog/gay-christian-network-conference.

19. Stoyan Zaimov, "Christian Publisher of Matthew Vines' 'God and the Gay Christian' Responds to NRB Resignation," *Christian Post*, May 24, 2014, christianpost.com/news/christian-publisher-of-matthew-vines-god-and-the-gay-christian-responds-to-nrb-resignation-120043/#WG6sQSiExpx8xoex.99.

20. See gaychristian.net.

21. See gaychristianonline.org.

22. See gaysforjesus.com.

23. Mike Oppenheimer, "What Does John Mean When He Writes *Whosoever Is Born of God Does Not Commit Sin*," Let Us Reason Ministries, 2009, accessed December 28, 2015, letusreason.org/Biblexp55.htm.

24. Martin Luther, as quoted in Robert Jamieson, Andrew Robert Fausset, and David Brown, commentary on 1 John 3, *Commentary Critical and Explanatory on the Whole Bible* (nineteenth century), on Study Light, accessed December 28, 2015, studylight.org/commentaries/jfb/view.cgi?bk=61&ch=3.

25. Evans, "Unstoppable Grace."

26. Nothstine, "Tony Campolo."

27. David Gushee, as quoted in Merritt, "David Gushee."

28. Adrian Rodgers, excerpts from presentation at National Religious Broadcasters Convention, 1996, as quoted in Puritan Board, October 23, 2005, puritanboard.com/showthread.php/9758-A-good-quote-regarding-truth.

29. Tony Campolo, *Speaking My Mind: The Radical Evangelical Prophet Tackles the Tough Issues Christians Are Afraid to Face* (Nashville: W Publishing, 2004), 72.

30. Nothstine, "Tony Campolo."

31. Mary Jacobs, "Q&A with Chuck Smith Jr.," *Dallas Morning News*, December 10, 2005, as quoted on Religion News Blog, December 11, 2005, religionnewsblog.com/14301/qa-with-chuck-smith-jr.

32. Chuck Smith Jr., in video "Building Bridges, Part IV," Evangelical Network, November 18, 2010, bing.com/videos/search?q=youtube+chuck+smith+jr+gays&view=detail&mid=72DB8642EE15CB82CD5472DB8642EE15CB82CD54&FORM=VIRE9.

33. Brian McLaren, as quoted in "Brian McLaren on the Homosexual Question: Finding a Pastoral Response," *Leadership Journal*, January 2006, christianitytoday.com/le/2006/january-online-only/brian-mclaren-on-homosexual-question-finding-pastoral.html.

34. Brian McLaren, as quoted in Tony Jones, "Brian McLaren's View."

35. C. S. Lewis, *The Problem of Pain* (1940; repr., New York: HarperCollins, 2001), 47.

36. Paul Morris, *Shadow of Sodom* (Wheaton: Tyndale House, 1978), 89.

Chapter 9 Sodom

1. Boswell, *Christianity, Social Tolerance, and Homosexuality*, 93–98.

2. Matthew Vines, *God and the Gay Christian* (New York: Convergent Books, 2014), 67.

3. Robin Scroggs, *The New Testament and Homosexuality* (Philadelphia: Fortress, 1983), 13–14.

4. Rick Brentlinger, "The Sin of Sodom according to Jesus Was NOT Homosexuality," Gay Christian 101, accessed December 30, 2015, gaychristian101.com/Sin-of-Sodom.html.

5. B. A. Robinson, "Why Did God Destroy the City of Sodom and Its People?," Religious Tolerance, February 29, 2012, religioustolerance.org/hombibg193.htm.

6. John J. McNeil, *The Church and the Homosexual* (Boston: Beacon Press, 1993), 50.

7. Vines, *God and the Gay Christian*, 67.

8. Boswell, *Christianity, Social Tolerance, and Homosexuality*, 96.

9. David Gushee, "The Sins of Sodom: The LGBT Issue, Part 9," *Baptist News*, September 2, 2014, baptistnews.com/opinion/columns/item/29133-the-sins-of-sodom-and-gibeah-the-lgbt-issue-part-9.

10. Vines, *God and the Gay Christian*, 69.

11. Robert Gagnon, *The Bible and Homosexual Practice: Texts and Hermeneutics* (Nashville: Abingdon, 2001), 87.

12. Boswell, *Christianity, Social Tolerance, and Homosexuality*, 94.

13. Derrick Bailey, *Homosexuality and the Western Christian Tradition* (London: Shoe String Press, 1955), 2–3.

14. Thomas Schmidt, *Straight and Narrow? Compassion and Clarity in the Homosexual Debate* (Downers Grove, IL: InterVarsity, 1995), 89.

15. Gagnon, *Bible and Homosexual Practice*, 71.

16. Schmidt, *Straight and Narrow?*, 88–89.

17. Gagnon, *Bible and Homosexual Practice*, 79, emphasis added.

18. Greg Koukl, "What Was the Sin of Sodom and Gomorrah?" Stand to Reason, March 8, 2013, str.org/articles/what-was-the-sin-of-sodom-and-gomorrah#.VeurfzhRGP8.

Chapter 10 Homosexuality and Leviticus

1. Transcribed from the *West Wing* episode 2.3, "The Midterms," aired October 18, 2000, on West Wing Transcripts, accessed December 30, 2015, westwingtranscripts.com/search.php?flag=getTranscript&id=25&keyword=The Midterms.

2. Tom Horner, *Jonathan Loved David: Homosexuality in Biblical Times* (Philadelphia: Westminster, 1978), 71.

3. Troy Perry, *Don't Be Afraid Anymore* (New York: St. Martin's, 1990), 40.

4. Marc Shaiman, "Prop 8—The Musical," YouTube video, 3:20, posted by Funny or Die, October 31, 2009, youtube.com/watch?v=B_hyT7_Bx9o.

5. Vines, *God and the Gay Christian*, 78.

6. Greg Koukl, "How Does the Old Testament Law Apply to Christians Today?," Stand to Reason, April 28, 2014, str.org/articles/how-does-the-old-testament-law-apply-to-christians-today#.Vd_WFjhRGP9.

7. Gagnon, *Bible and Homosexual Practice*, 128.

8. Justin Lee, *Torn* (New York: Jericho Books, 2012), 177.

9. John MacArthur, *The MacArthur Bible Commentary* (Nashville: Thomas Nelson, 2005), 1038, as quoted in Rick Brentlinger, "Shrine Prostitutes—Is THAT What Moses Was Talking about in Leviticus 18:22 and 20:30?," Gay Christian 101, revised August 24, 2015, gaychristian101.com/Shrine-Prostitutes.html.

10. Gagnon, *Bible and Homosexual Practice*, 130.

11. Boswell, *Christianity, Social Tolerance, and Homosexuality*, 100–102; Horner, *Jonathan Loved David*, 73.

12. Boswell, *Christianity, Social Tolerance, and Homosexuality*, 100.

13. Vines, *God and the Gay Christian*, 85.

14. Ibid.

15. Gerald Sheppard, "The Use of Scripture within the Christian Ethical Debate Concerning Same-Sex Oriented Persons," *Union Seminary Quarterly Review* 40 (1985), as quoted in Gagnon, *Bible and Homosexual Practice,* 131.

16. William Loader, *The New Testament on Sexuality* (Grand Rapids: Eerdmans, 2012), 25.

17. Gagnon, *Bible and Homosexual Practice*, 131.

18. Ibid., 118–19.

19. Ibid.

20. See Hebrew entry number 6945, *Strong's Concordance*, Bible Hub Online Bible Study Suite, accessed December 28, 2015, biblehub.com/hebrew/6945.htm.

21. James Neill, *The Origins and Role of Same-Sex Relations in Human Societies* (Jefferson, NC: McFarland, 2011), 110–13.

22. Sean McDowell, "Does the Levitical Prohibition of Homosexuality Still Apply Today?" *Christian Research Journal* 38 no. 2 (2015): 45.

23. Don Bromley, "Don Bromley Response to Bible Text Discussion," Think Theology, July 24, 2013, thinktheology.org/wp-content/uploads/2014/04/Don-Bromley-Response-to-Bible-Text-Discussion.pdf.

24. Philo, as quoted in Scroggs, *New Testament and Homosexuality*, 88.

25. Scroggs, *New Testament and Homosexuality*, 88.

26. Robert Gagnon, "An Open Letter to Justin Lee, Author of *Torn*: I Do Not Believe Lev 18:22 and 20:13 Indict Only Idolatrous Forms of Homosexual Practice," Patheos, March 28, 2013, patheos.com/blogs/philosophicalfragments/2013/03/28/bible-condemn-idolatrous-homosexual-practice-gangnon-lee-torn.

27. Vines, *God and the Gay Christian*, 86.

28. Ibid., 88.

29. Ibid.

30. Ibid., 87.

31. Philo, *Philo* 3.39; 7.499, trans. F. H. Colson (Cambridge, MA: Harvard University Press, 1954), as quoted in "The Special Laws," Born Eunuchs, 2001, accessed January 2, 2016, well.com/user/aquarius/philo-speciallaws.htm.

32. Aristides, "The Apology of Aristides the Philosopher," as quoted in Peter Kirby, "Historical Jesus Theories," Early Christian Writings, accessed December 30, 2015, earlychristianwritings.com/text/aristides-kay.html.

33. Athenagoras, "A Plea for the Christians," trans. B. P. Pratten, as quoted in Darren L. Slider, Logos Virtual Library, accessed January 3, 2016, logoslibrary.org/athenagoras/plea/34.html.

34. See Justin Martyr, *Second Apology 12,* AD 150–157, revised and edited by Kevin Knight, "The 2nd Apology of St. Justin Martyr," New Advent, 2000, accessed January 2, 2016, www.newadvent.org/fathers/0127.htm.

35. See Theophilus, "To Autolycus," book I, chapter 2, as quoted in Harry Plantinga, Christian Classics Ethereal Library, accessed January 2, 2016, ccel.org/ccel/schaff/anf02.iv.ii.iii.x.html.

36. See Origen, *Against Celsus,* book VII, chapter 49, AD 248, as quoted in Peter Kirby, Early Christian Writings, accessed January 2, 2016, earlychristianwritings.com/text/origen167.html.

37. Ibid., 46.

38. Gagnon, *Bible and Homosexual Practice*, 145.

Chapter 11 What Jesus Did or Did Not Say

1. Michael F. Haverluck, "WWJD? Jimmy Carter Says Support 'Gay Marriage,' Abortion," One News Now, July 13, 2015, onenewsnow.com/politics-govt/2015/07/13/wwjd -jimmy-carter-says-support-gay-marriage-abortion.

2. Ben Johnson, "Obama Endorses Gay 'Marriage': Says Support Based on Jesus, Golden Rule," Life Site, May 9, 2012, lifesitenews.com/news/obama-says-his-support -for-same-sex-marriage-based-on-the-golden-rule.

3. Perry, *Don't Be Afraid Anymore*, 341.

4. "What Jesus Says about Homosexuality," *Huffington Post*, January 22, 2013, huffington post.com/2013/12/22/what-jesus-says-about-homosexuality-_n_4489452.html.

5. Cynthia Clawson, "A Personal Mission Statement from Cynthia Clawson," Gay Christian Movement Watch, May 14, 2008, gcmwatch.com/443/cynthia-clawson.

6. Jay Michaelson, "When Jesus Healed a Same-Sex Partner," *Huffington Post*, August 7, 2012, huffingtonpost.com/jay-michaelson/when-jesus-healed-a-same-sex-partner _b_1743947.html.

7. John Byron, "Did Jesus Heal a Centurion's Same-Sex Partner?," The Biblical World, August 9, 2012, thebiblicalworld.blogspot.com/2012/08/did-jesus-heal-centurions -same-sex.html.

8. Ibid.

9. Horner, *Jonathan Loved David*, 122.

10. "Jesus Affirmed a Gay Couple," LifeJourney Church's website, Would Jesus Discriminate?, accessed December 28, 2015, wouldjesusdiscriminate.org/biblical_evidence /gay_couple.html.

11. Kenneth Dover, *Greek Homosexuality* (Cambridge, MA: Harvard University Press, 1997), 16.

12. Michaelson, "When Jesus Healed a Same-Sex Partner."

13. Donald Meder, "The *Entimos Pais* of Matthew 8:5–13 and Luke 7:1–10," *Paideka: The Journal of Paedophilia* 1, no. 1 (1987): 27–39.

14. Robert Gagnon, "Did Jesus Approve of a Homosexual Couple in the Story of the Centurion at Capernaum?," RobGagnon.net, April 24, 2007, robgagnon.net/Homosex CenturionStory.htm.

15. Horner, *Jonathan Loved David*, 123–24.

16. Clement of Alexandria, as quoted in Mark Brustman, "The Ancient Roman and Talmudic Definition of Natural Eunuchs," Born Eunuchs, July 27, 1999, well.com/user /aquarius/cardiff.htm.

17. BGEA staff, "Q: Does the Bible Approve of Some Homosexual Relationships?," Billy Graham Evangelistic Association, June 1, 2004, billygraham.org/answer/does-the -bible-approve-of-some-homosexual-relationships.

Chapter 12 Paul and Romans

1. Vines, *God and the Gay Christian*, 96.

2. Johnson, "Obama Endorses Gay 'Marriage.'"

3. Bennett J. Sims, "Say 'Yes' to Same-Sex Unions While Being True to the Bible," *Aisling* 25 (1999), aislingmagazine.com/aislingmagazine/articles/TAM25/SayYes.html.

4. Boswell, *Christianity, Social Tolerance, and Homosexuality*, 109.

5. Scanzoni and Mollenkott, *Is the Homosexual My Neighbor?*, 65–66.

6. James Cunningham, "Romans Chapter 1: Are Homosexuals Just Perverted Heterosexuals?," Gay Christian Survivors, accessed December 28, 2015, gaychristiansurvivors .tripod.com/id9.html.

7. B. A. Robinson, "Antigay 'Clobber' Passages in the Bible: Introduction to Romans 1:26–27," Religious Tolerance, March 4, 2012, religioustolerance.org/hom_bibc3.htm.

8. Matthew Vines, "The Gay Debate: The Bible and Homosexuality," Matthew Vines, accessed December 28, 2015, matthewvines.com/transcript.

9. William Schoedel, as quoted in Robert Gagnon, "On Boswell and 'Men Who Lie with a Male' in 1 Corinthians 6:9: A Response to Harwood and Porter regarding Material Posted on Presbyweb on June 23 and June 25, 2004," RobGagnon.net, June 30, 2004, robgagnon.net/RespHarwoodPorter.htm.

10. Bernadette Brooten, *Love between Women: Early Christian Responses to Female Homoeroticism* (Chicago: University of Chicago Press, 1998), 244.

11. Jeff Allen, "The Apostle Paul and Homosexuality—Answering Homosexual Objections (Part 2)," *Charisma News*, June 5, 2014, charismanews.com/opinion/44135-the -apostle-paul-and-homosexuality-answering-homosexual-objections-part-2?showall=1.

12. Vines, *God and the Gay Christian*, 105.

13. Dio Chrysostom, as quoted in Vines, *God and the Gay Christian*, 104–5.

14. Entry for *aselgeia*, *NAS New Testament Greek Lexicon*, as published on Bible Study Tools, accessed January 2, 2016, biblestudytools.com/lexicons/greek/nas/aselgeia.html.

15. Vines, *God and the Gay Christian*, 105.

16. Perry, *Don't Be Afraid Anymore*, 342.

17. "Idol Worship and Rejection of God (Romans 1:21–28)," LifeJourney Church's website, Would Jesus Discriminate?, accessed December 28, 2015, wouldjesusdiscriminate .org/biblical_evidence/romans_1_21.html.

18. Justin Lee, "The Great Debate," Gay Christian Network, accessed December 28, 2015, gaychristian.net/justins_view.php.

19. Jack Rogers, "God and Homosexuality: Part 5—Romans 1," Word of a Woman, April 3, 2012, wordofawoman.com/tag/jack-rogers.

20. Schmidt, *Straight and Narrow?*, 78–79.

21. Robert Gagnon, "Does Jack Rogers's Book 'Explode the Myths' about the Bible and Homosexuality and 'Heal the Church'?" Installment 3, RobGagnon.net, June 10, 2006, 3, robgagnon.net/articles/RogersBookReviewed3.pdf.

22. Ibid.

23. Bromley, "Don Bromley Response."

24. Oliver Buzz, "When Religion Loses Its Credibility," *USA Today*, November 19, 2006, usatoday30.usatoday.com/news/opinion/editorials/2006-11-19-forum-religion _x.htm.

25. Arland J. Hultgren, "Being Faithful to the Scriptures: Romans 1:26–27 as a Case in Point," Seminary Forum, *Word & World*, 14, no. 3 (Summer 1994), Luther Seminary, St. Paul, Minnesota, wordandworld.luthersem.edu/content/pdfs/14-3_Sex/14-3 _Hultgren.pdf.

26. Scroggs, *New Testament and Homosexuality*, 116.

27. Ibid., 35–36.
28. Jack Rogers, *Jesus, the Bible, and Homosexuality: Explode the Myths, Heal the Church*, rev. ed. (Louisville: Westminster John Knox, 2009), 58.
29. Plato, *Symposium*, trans. Benjamin Jowett, as published by Daniel C. Stevenson, The Internet Classics Archives, accessed January 2, 2016, classics.mit.edu/Plato/symposium.1b.txt.
30. As summarized in Gip Plaster, "Bernardette Brooten: Love between Women," The Gayscribe Archive, April 7, 2012, gayscribe.com/betweenwomen.
31. Thomas K. Hubbard, *Homosexuality in Greece and Rome: A Sourcebook of Basic Documents* (Berkeley: University of California Press, 2003), 386, emphasis added.
32. Quency E. Wallace, "The Early Life and Background of Paul the Apostle," *American Journal of Biblical Theology* 3, no. 8 (April 21, 2002), biblicaltheology.com/Research/WallaceQ01.html.
33. "Paul and His Use of Greek Philosophy," Bible Things in Bible Ways, July 14, 2013, biblethingsinbibleways.wordpress.com/2013/07/14/paul-and-his-use-of-greek-philosophy.
34. Albert Mohler, "God, the Gospel, and the Gay Challenge—A Response to Matthew Vines," AlbertMohler.com, April 22, 2014, albertmohler.com/2014/04/22/god-the-gospel-and-the-gay-challenge-a-response-to-matthew-vines.
35. Ibid.

Chapter 13 Paul and *Arsenokoitēs*

1. Gary F. Zeolla, "'Homosexuals' in 1 Corinthians 6:9," Darkness to Light, March 19, 1998, dtl.org/ethics/article/homosexuals.htm.
2. Timothy Dailey, *The Bible, Church, and Homosexuality* (Washington, DC: Family Research Council, 2004), 11.
3. See Roger Nicole, "New Testament Use of the Old Testament," *Revelation and the Bible*, ed. Carl F. H. Henry (Grand Rapids: Baker, 1958), 137–51.
4. Louis Crompton, *Homosexuality and Civilization* (Boston: Belknap Press of Harvard University, 2003), 80.
5. Dale B. Martin, as quoted in William Birch, "Malakoi, Arsenokoitai, and the Homosexual," William Birch l'Épiscopalien, December 3, 2014, http://www.williambirch.net/2014/12/malakoi-arsenokoitai-and-homosexual.html.
6. Vines, *God and the Gay Christian*, 130.
7. Rick Brentlinger, "*Arsenokoites*—What Is the Historical Meaning of This Rare Greek Word?," Gay Christian 101, accessed January 2, 2016, gaychristian101.com/Arsenokoites.html.
8. B. A. Robinson, "Meanings of the Greek Word *Arsenokoitai*," Religious Tolerance, May 16, 2011, religioustolerance.org/homarsen.htm.
9. Mel White, "What the Bible Says—and Doesn't Say—about Homosexuality," Soulforce, 16, accessed December 28, 2015, psa91.com/pdf/whatthebiblesays.pdf.
10. Rick Brentlinger, "Define *Arsenokoitēs*: This Word DID NOT Refer to Homosexual in Ancient Usage," Gay Christian 101, April 7, 2014, gaychristian101.com/Define-Arsenokoites.html.
11. Boswell, *Christianity, Social Tolerance, and Homosexuality*.
12. Ibid., 341.

13. Ibid., 344.

14. Ibid.

15. Vines, *God and the Gay Christian*, 124–26; Dale Martin, *Sex and the Single Savior: Gender and Sexuality in Biblical Interpretation* (Louisville: Westminster John Knox, 2006), 42.

16. Leon Morris, as quoted in Brentlinger, "*Arsenokoitēs.*"

17. Charles Eerdman, as quoted in Brentlinger, "*Arsenokoitēs.*"

18. Phil Johnson, as quoted in Brentlinger, "*Arsenokoitēs.*"

19. Robert Gagnon, "Bad Reasons for Changing One's Mind: Jack Rogers's Temple Prostitution Argument and Other False Starts," RobGagnon.net, March 1, 2004, 2, robgagnon.net/articles/homoRogersResp2.pdf.

20. Bruce Metzger, *The Bible in Translation* (Grand Rapids: Baker, 2001), 18.

21. David F. Wright, "Homosexuals or Prostitutes? The Meaning of *Arsenokoitai*," *Vigiliae Christianae* 38 (1984): 356, williamapercy.com/wiki/images/Homosexuals_or _prostitutes_studies_of_homosexuality_volume_12.pdf.

22. S.v. "pornos," Strong's Concordance on Blue Letter Bible website, 2016, https://www .blueletterbible.org/lang/Lexicon/Lexicon.cfm?strongs=G4205&t=KJV.

23. Gagnon, "Bad Reasons," 2.

24. Ross Taylor, as quoted in Jason R. Velotta, "Who Are the *Arsenokoitai* Which Are Excluded from the Kingdom of God in 1 Corinthians 6:9?" paper for Temple Baptist Seminary, Brownsville, TN, March 2010, 23, christchurchofbrownsville.com/arsenokoitai _final_paper.doc.

Chapter 14 When It's All Said and Done

1. Grandma (Helen Shaw), *Parenthood*, dir. by Ron Howard (Universal Pictures, 1989), cited on IMDb, imdb.com/character/ch0155310/quotes.

A former gay activist, **Joe Dallas** is a pastoral counselor and the author of seven books on human sexuality from a biblical perspective. A contributing writer for the *Christian Research Journal*, he has also written for *Christianity Today*, the *Conversations* journal of the Christian Association of Psychological Studies (CAPS), *Cornerstone* magazine, Focus on the Family's *Citizen Magazine*, and several other publications. He has appeared on the ABC *Evening News*, *The Bible Answer Man*, *Focus on the Family*, *The 700 Club*, *The Laura Ingram Show*, *Janet Parshall Live*, and many other media outlets. A popular speaker at men's conferences, he speaks regularly in the US and worldwide.

CONNECT WITH
JOE DALLAS

JOE DALLAS ONLINE BLOG

Joe Dallas Online is a blog for men striving to attain and maintain sexual integrity. It is a specifically Christian site, though everyone is welcome regardless of belief or worldview.

http://joedallas.com/blog/

🐦 @JoeDallasTGP
f Facebook.com/JoeDallasOnline